Green River

Thompson

GREEN RIVER STATE PARK

Devils Garden

ARCHES NATIONAL PARK

UTAH

Delicate Arch

Colorado River

Dolores River

The Windows

Moab

CANYONLANDS NATIONAL PARK

Island in the Sky El. 6,000 Ft.

CANYONLANDS NATIONAL PARK

DEAD HORSE POINT STATE PARK

La Sal Mountains

Mt. Peale El. 12,721 Ft.

La Sal

Green River

Grand View Point

Needles Overlook

Colorado River

The Maze

Confluence of Green and Colorado Rivers

Dirty Devil River

Orange Cliffs

GLEN CANYON NATIONAL RECREATION AREA

The Doll House

The Needles

Cataract Canyon

NEWSPAPER ROCK STATE HISTORICAL MON.

Hite

EN NYON ATIONAL RECREATION EA

Abajo Mountains

Monticello

Abajo Peak El. 11,360 Ft.

95

Fry Canyon

NATURAL BRIDGES NATIONAL MONUMENT

EDGE OF THE CEDARS STATE PARK

Blanding

Pleasant View

95

276

HOVENWEEP NATIONAL MONUMENT

261

Cortez

160

262

VALLEY OF THE GODS

191

Bluff

an River

GOOSENECKS STATE PARK

Mexican Hat

191

163

Four Corners Monument

95

MONUMENT VALLEY NAVAJO TRIBAL PARK

UTAH COLORADO

ARIZONA NEW MEXICO

"As the greatest
expanse of exposed
rock in North America,
the slickrock canyon
country reveals sagas
of the earth's history
that would otherwise
be virtually unknown.
...A sense of
discovery can still
be kindled here."

GARY PAUL NABHAN
AND CAROLINE WILSON

CANYONS
UTAH'S SLICK

GARY PAUL NABHAN

PHOTOGRAPHY

HarperCollins*West* *A Division of HarperCollinsPublishers*

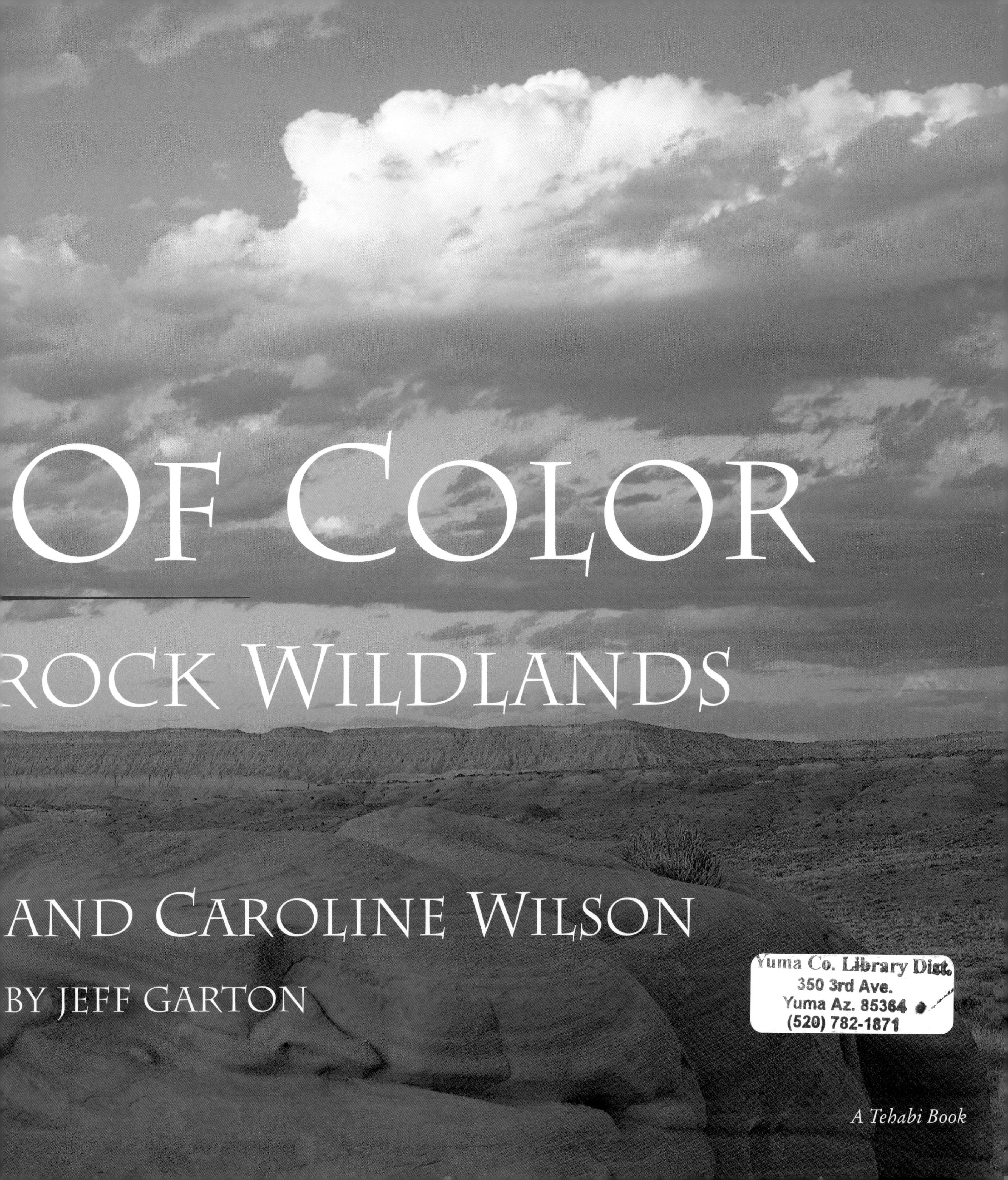

OF COLOR

ROCK WILDLANDS

AND CAROLINE WILSON

BY JEFF GARTON

A Tehabi Book

DEDICATION

This book is dedicated to the memory of Bates Wilson, a one-of-a-kind man with sand in his soul, and to the other Wilsons who supported his work: Edie, Tug, Julie, Robin, Lynn, Anne, and Speck.

The Genesis Series was conceived by Tehabi Books and published by HarperCollins*West*. The series celebrates the epic geologic processes that created and continue to shape America's magnificent national parks and their distinctive ecosystems. The books are written by some of the nation's most evocative nature writers and feature images from some of the best nature photographers in the world.

Canyons of Color: Utah's Slickrock Wildlands was produced by Tehabi Books. Susan Wels, *Genesis Series Editor;* Jeff Campbell, *Copy Editor;* Anne Hayes, *Copy Proofer;* Nancy Cash, *Managing Editor;* Tom Lewis, *Editorial and Design Director;* Sharon Lewis, *Controller;* Chris Capen, *President.*

Written by Gary Paul Nabhan and Caroline Wilson, *Canyons of Color* features the photography of Jeff Garton with supplemental photography provided by Tom and Pat Leeson (pages 99, 100, 106c and 107d). Technical, 3-D illustrations were produced by Sam Lewis. Source materials for the illustrations were provided as digital elevation models from the United States Geological Survey. Additional illustrations were produced by Andy Lewis and Tom Lewis.

For more information on Utah's slickrock wildlands, HarperCollins*West* and Tehabi Books encourage readers to contact the Canyonlands Natural History Association, 30 South 100 East, Moab, Utah 84532; (801) 259-6003.

HarperCollins*West* and Tehabi Books, in association with The Basic Foundation, a not-for-profit organization whose primary mission is reforestation, will facilitate the planting of two trees for every one tree used in the manufacture of this book.

Library of Congress Cataloging-in-Publication Data
Nabhan, Gary Paul
   Canyons of Color : Utah's slickrock wildlands / Gary Nabhan and Caroline Wilson. — 1st ed.
   p. cm. — (Genesis series)
  Includes index.
  ISBN 0-06-258571-1 (cloth). — ISBN 0-06-258560-6 (paperback)
1. Canyons — Utah — Pictorial works. 2. Utah — Pictorial works. 3. Red beds — Utah — Pictorial works. 4. Red beds — Utah. 5. Utah — Description and Travel. I. Wilson, Caroline C. II. Title. III. Series: Genesis series.
F827.N33 1995
917.92`59`009144-dc20
                                                      94-24059
                                                          CIP

95 96 97 98 TBI 10 9 8 7 6 5 4 3 2 1

This edition is printed on acid-free paper that meets the American National Standards Institute Z39.48 Standard.

THE GENESIS SERIES

CANYONS OF COLOR

UTAH'S SLICKROCK WILDLANDS

Caroline remembers: I grew up in a fault. I didn't know it at the time, at least not in my earliest years as a "park brat" at Arches National Park, where my father was the Superintendent from 1949 to 1971. I suspected there was something special about the canyon we lived in, but I didn't understand why everyone was always looking up and pointing to its towering red rock walls.

We often had guests for dinner at our rock house at the Arches headquarters, which was built by the Civilian Conservation Corps. Sometimes our guests were photographers, geologists, or archaeologists who had come to study the canyon country, but other times they were just friends from out of town who had come for camping and Jeep trips. During happy hour, my father loved to take our guests outside to explain the geological wonder of the Moab Fault. Everyone would follow him out the front door, drinks in hand, and listen as he mesmerized them with the story of what had happened there over fifty million years ago. They would tilt their heads, stare, and blink, as if trying to comprehend some strange evening news. I remember much pointing, arm waving, questions, answers, and finally, the oohs and aahs.

Soon all the guests would understand that one side of the valley had gone up while the other side had dropped down, resulting in some two thousand feet of displacement! "And so, the Wingate sandstone, up there, should sit under the Navajo, right over here at eye level. . ." my

This canyon, its walls streaked with desert varnish, feeds into the Escalante River, a tributary of the Colorado. It is one of thousands of canyons that crisscross the landscape of southeast Utah.

BETWEEN CLIFF WALLS

CANYON COUNTRY DEFINED

father would explain, one hand in his jeans pocket and the other lifting his Jim Beam to the sky in the direction of the great Wingate Cliffs. Our guests would turn like clockwork when he shifted to point at the rocks just behind us. Even if they had a hard time fathoming that much rock being moved around, Bates Wilson's broad smile and easy tone could convince them that such an event actually happened. My sister and I watched as our father told this story dozens of times, not sure what the big deal was, but happy that everyone admired our backyard rocks.

Years later, she and I returned to the rocky playground of our childhood. As adults, we had begun to take some interest in the geologic story of Utah, so we stopped along the entrance road into Arches and took a fresh look at our old home canyon. With one eye on the cliffs and the other on the geologic map, at last, we saw the fault line, the dipping strata, and understood. Wishing we could share our discovery with our father, who had long since passed away, we turned to each other. There was silence between us, and a breeze whistled high up in the cliffs. "So this is what he would get so excited about!" one of us offered to the wind. And his excitement was now our own.

* * *

Gary remembers: I was seventeen and skinny then, a few weeks before I left school to work for Earth Day Headquarters in March of 1970. It would be my first backpack into a desert wilderness, whose dimensions I could hardly grasp. The station wagon was loaded with students from a Midwestern corn town, and most of us had never seen so little green and so much rock in all our lives. After driving two days and nights, we paused at the petroglyphs on Newspaper Rock just as darkness seeped into the canyon. We tried in vain to decipher the meaning of the dancing figures and mating bighorn. We drove on for another half hour and arrived at Squaw Flat Campground in the six-year-old Canyonlands National Park.

After unpacking gear in the blackness and setting up tents, someone suggested we make a little fire to warm our hands. That was when I made my first mistake: while groping for kindling, I pulled down a branch of a juniper tree I thought to be dead. The ancient, gnarled mass looked like no living thing I had ever seen. It seemed to growl at me.

My second mistake came a half hour later—unrolling my sleeping bag out on some odd, dark, crusty soil. I had no idea that I was crushing hundred-year-old lichen and cyanobacteria, the living mass I now call "cryptobiotic crust." In the morning when I saw more cryptobiotic soil, I wrote in my notes how it looked like a miniature version of the rock spires around us. A ranger explained that the stuff is as alive as you or me. I now treat the cryptos as elders the same way I do the junipers.

The next night I made my third mistake—snuggling down in the soft sand of a desert wash (this time to avoid the cryptos). A storm swept up on us in the middle of the night, and I had a nightmare that the desert had been transformed into a tempestuous ocean. Some wet dream: I was awakened by the flow of floodwater under my sleeping bag. We quickly packed up our soggy gear and moved to higher ground.

The Penguins, carved from the slick-rock member of the Entrada sandstone in Arches National Park, stand guard over the Moab Fault. The Wingate sandstone cliffs on the far side of the canyon should rightfully sit below the Penguins, but the fault caused over two thousand feet of displacement: the Penguins' side of the canyon went down while the other side went up.

FOLLOWING PAGES:

The Hoodoo Entrada, a silty version of the Entrada sandstone, contrasts sharply with the white Curtis formation, rock of marine origin, above it. This view is in the South Desert, Capitol Reef National Park.

As I learned a few of the land's rules and came to feel comfortable carrying a backpack across slickrock, the next few days were rich with discoveries. I noticed that the reds and grays and tans overwhelmed any greenery tucked in cracks in the rock. The lack of human scale was disorienting and humbling. I had to fully engage my hands, soles, toes, and mind in order to slither up chimneys and joints in the sandstone or to slide down shale slopes still slick as gumbo with the recent rains. But I had an inkling that I could fit quite well into the canyon country, given enough time to learn more of its idiosyncracies.

The country engaged me like no other place had ever done. Something was conceived then that had not been part of my life until I entered those canyons of color. Within nine months I had left the Midwest for good and moved to the arid Southwest, where I remain today.

Two weeks after coming west, I had another dream. I imagined that the dryness had blistered most of the skin off my bones, that my ribs had begun to show, a tanned, leathery hide stretched miserably over them. "Look within and adjust the mechanism of perception," a wilderness mentor wrote me at that time. I was shedding old presumptions about the world as I knew it. The frugal cacti and cacophonous ravens were becoming my new mentors.

* * *

Caroline and Gary remember: Looking back at those early impressions of Utah's rugged wildlands, we can now see how they captivated us both. Our ears have become familiar with a lexicon distinct from cityspeak, and we've unconsciously absorbed a repertoire of sounds unique to the canyons of color. We have let the cascading song of the canyon wren shape the rhythm of the way we breathe. We have shaken with the echo of crashing rockslide, and we've memorized the sound of wind in the pinyon pine.

The pages that follow are filled with the sounds and shapes of this special place. It is a land loaded with goblins and hoodoos, fins and needles, measle rock and mushrooms. It is carpeted by old man sage, shadscale, kachina daisies, Brigham tea, Moenkopi milk vetch, Navajo sedge, Whipple's fishhook cactus, alcove death camas, Apache plume, and dune broom. It is peopled by canyon mice and desert bighorn, Clark's nutcrackers and white-tailed prairie dogs, black phoebes, and kangaroo rats. Its spirit reverberates with the songs of the Fremont, Anasazi, Navajo, Ute, Southern Paiute, Spanish explorers, and Mormon battalions.

* * *

Viewed from the air, the slickrock wildlands are a vividly colored spot on the face of the earth. The reds, oranges, buffs, purples, peaches, and pinks of this country form a cohesive region—what geographers call the Canyonlands section of the Colorado Plateau. Each of those hues hints at a different geological episode, and each rock layer favors a particular bunch of tenacious plants. Even before visitors to canyon country learn the names of its key plants, animals, and geologic features, most can grasp some immediate sense of the unique ecologic stage on which its lifeforms act and interact.

T*he canyon country term "slickrock" refers to an expanse of solid rock that forms a nearly flat platform or bench, like this exposure of White Rim sandstone in Canyonlands National Park.*

As the greatest expanse of exposed rock in North America, the slickrock canyon country reveals sagas of the earth's history that would otherwise be virtually unknown. Even when plant cover is lush after spring snowmelts or summer rain, it seldom covers more than a fourth of the ground surface, so you can usually see the geologic backbone of the land. As one rock jock once quipped, "Up here, there isn't enough green stuff to spoil your view of what matters."

This wilderness of rock, with its near-vertical cliff walls, forms an impenetrable backdrop that dwarfs any human construct. Passage is limited to a few circuitous routes through the maze of sheer canyons. The bywords "Ya cain't get there from here" apply more often than not in the wilds of southeast Utah.

*D*rained by the Colorado River and its tributaries, the Colorado Plateau consists of a high, broad tableland of largely flat-lying, sedimentary rocks. It has eroded into many smaller plateaus and basins, outlined by stairsteps of cliffs. The plateau country is distinct in that most of its rock layers remain in the same horizontal position in which they were laid down, unlike other, neighboring regions where the rock has been warped and folded by mountain-building forces.

THE COLORADO PLATEAU

And, remarkably, the most prominent feature of this arid landscape—the canyon—has been created by the erosive action of water. The paradox doesn't stop there: hidden within the canyons—in country that receives only five to nine inches of rain per year—are alcoves with dripping springs, riparian corridors lined with willows, and hanging gardens lush with monkeyflowers and maidenhair ferns.

A sense of discovery can still be kindled here, even though the canyon country was first "discovered" by humans over twelve thousand years ago. European-American explorers have been writing about its "unknown corners" since Juan Maria Antonio de Rivera entered Paradox Valley west of Moab in 1765. Parts of it may have looked unpopulated to him, but eight hundred to nine hundred years ago, when Fremont and Anasazi Indians occupied its canyons and mesas, the Colorado Plateau harbored twice its modern population. You may unexpectedly stumble upon their petroglyphs, potsherds, or granaries in a place not previously recorded. Running the Colorado, Green, or San Juan Rivers can also carry with it a never-ending supply of natural—and unnatural—surprises. As a local rancher,

Pine Tree Arch is one of many arches found in Arches National Park, which preserves the greatest number of natural arches in the world.

Doc Tangren, muttered when he saw river-runner Kent Frost take a couple from Chicago down the Green River on a homemade raft, "Never thought I'd see a woman come down a river on a thing like that. I'd say it was a good way to get rid of her!"

* * *

Since there is considerable variability in the landscapes of canyon country, many researchers—explorers and geographers, archaeologists and hydrologists, and ecologists and botanists—have spent years trying to define and delineate this place in a way that is to everyone's liking. Meantime, the rocks, ravens, and plants have kept on doing what they've always done, regardless of how they are lumped together on maps or surveys.

Satellite photos tell us one thing for sure about the geographic boundaries of canyon country: there's a huge patch of brilliantly colored, canyon-riddled rock between the Aquarius Plateau on the west and the La Sal Mountains to the east. The canyons of color between these uplifts extend northeast to the Book Cliffs and northwest to the San Rafael Swell. The San Juan River and Comb Ridge make a pretty good boundary in the southeast, and Monument Valley lies dead center in the southern reaches of the slickrock wildlands. For the southwest corner, take your pick: Glen Canyon or the southern end of Lake Powell. Whatever the case, the higher country of the Kaiparowits Plateau and the uplands of Zion are beyond our canyon country's horizon.

Other than geographic ties, what other common threads run through this country of crimson cliffs and canyons? For starters, drainage. The area encompasses all the tributaries of Utah's stretch of the Colorado River. These waterways drain a sweep of landscape over sixty miles in all directions from the confluence of the Colorado and its biggest tributary, the Green River.

Climate weaves another common thread. Canyon country precipitation is unpredictable and modest enough that most parts of the region are classified as arid or semiarid. Nevertheless, only the vegetation at lower elevations and droughty soils at midelevations can be classified as true desert, although most first-time visitors consider all of the canyon country to be a desert. The truth is, woodlands of pinyon-juniper, with their sage and grass meadowlands, cover as much surface as desert scrublands do. And above the pinyon-juniper zone, lush forests reach to nine thousand feet on four laccolithic mountain masses that tower above the canyons: Navajo Mountain and the La Sals, Henrys, and Abajos. As we figure it, there is as much pygmy woodland poker being played in canyon country as there is desert solitaire.

Other common threads, interlaced with those of climate, green and red rivers, and gnarled roots, run through this story. All the elevational ups and downs in canyon country have tended to rope off its flora and fauna from those of surrounding regions. Because natural geographic barriers have isolated plant life here for thousands of years, over seventy unique species live in the slickrock country. More endemic plants—those that grow in this area and nowhere else—are harbored here than in any other region in the West.

Natural bridges are formed when water carves a channel through solid rock. Sipapu Bridge is one of three bridges carved in the Cedar Mesa sandstone in Natural Bridges National Monument.

THE GREAT MONOCLINES:
IVORY RIPPLES ACROSS CANYON COUNTRY

T he folding and faulting activity of the Tertiary period, 66.4 to
1.5 million years ago, created
violent distortions of the earth's
surface in canyon country and
gave rise to the spectacular
monoclines—linear, sawtoothed
ridges of rock created by folds in
the earth's crust. Dramatic
canyon country monoclines
include San Rafael Reef, which
dips down like a frozen ocean
wave along the uplift known as
the San Rafael Swell; a jagged-edged monocline called Comb Ridge;
and Capitol Reef, a small section of a major overthrust called the
Waterpocket Fold. Draped with a cloak of white Navajo
sandstone, the canyon country's monoclines look
like great, ivory ripples on the landscape.

A long ridge of
Navajo sandstone along
Waterpocket Fold.

All these biogeographic threads come together in what we call "slickrock ecology." Each rock formation and the soils derived from it have their own peculiar chemistry, texture, and moisture-holding capacity. At the same time, the density, diversity, and stature of plants are all influenced by the characteristics of the parent materials on which they grow. This means each layer of the geological cake has a distinctive floral icing. For instance, although many kinds of plants can tolerate the conditions shared by sandstone and sandy dunes, others have difficulty growing on gypsum plugs, expansive clays, or fine-textured silts. Different mixes of plants and soils also favor different guilds of burrowing mammals, birds, and lizards.

Look at these chromatic rocks and tinted soils and the patterns of plants they support, add their attendant wildlife, and you can gain a sense of their landscape ecology—the relationships among them and the processes shaping their home: how plateaus are uplifted and canyons are downcut; how rivers meander and shales weather; how kangaroo rats resift the soil texture, which in turn favors some plants over others; and how beavers prune, puddle, dam, and build backwater homes along red rock rivers.

These are some of the tales from canyon country that echo between cliff walls. Close your eyes as you listen, and you can imagine the expansiveness and depth of this landscape. Its clefts, colors, and textures may become permanently etched into your mind's eye, for they are not easily forgotten.

FOLLOWING PAGES:

This view from Grand View Point, in the northern part of Canyonlands National Park, looks out across Monument Basin. The chocolate-brown pinnacles are sculpted from Organ Rock shale and are capped by a thin crust of White Rim sandstone.

*S*unrise at the Buttes
of the Cross and the
Green River. The Buttes
and vertical cliffs are
Wingate sandstone,
while the skirts below
are the uranium-rich
Chinle formation.

Soaked with color, the rock layers of canyon country have an aesthetic appeal to nearly everyone who has ever seen them. And yet, we never realized that stratigraphy (the layering of rock) could also serve as a babysitter until one time when we needed a new strategy for keeping the kids busy.

We had been camping and romping around southern Utah with friends for nearly two weeks when the children finally became bored. They had hiked, lizard-looped, run down dunes, and squeezed into hip-wide slot canyons. But in the evening back at camp they were restless. Then one of our friends said, "Hey kids, grab a plastic bag or a sock and come with me. Let's go make some presents for your friends."

From toddlers to ten year olds, all stopped and followed her over to a rainbow-colored slope.

"Who can fill a bag or sock with that purple clay over there? Can anyone reach the pinks? Can you crawl up to that green-gray ledge, dig down, and get some of the soft stuff under it?"

Within minutes, they were all back in camp pouring out piles of mauve, sienna, green, and pink shales onto flagstones. Using rounded rocks as their pestles, like Anasazi *manos* and *metates*, they ground each sediment down to a fine powder.

Each child took a clear bottle and poured in the color-rich sediments, layer upon layer—green on top of pink, turquoise on white, peach on mauve, gray over brown—until

The Chinle formation has its origins in wandering streams that flowed across open plains some 200 million years ago. Its hues range from lavender to shades of powder blue, buff, rust, and mauve. This slope of Chinle and the Wingate sandstone above it are in the Orange Cliffs.

LAYER UPON LAYER

A SEDIMENTARY SAGA

each had a geological parfait. A sand painting in a bottle.

"My colors look like the hills over there," a four-year-old exclaimed. She was right. Stratigraphy. The essence of geology. Layer upon layer.

Seas and Streams: The Paleozoic Era

Throughout most of the Colorado Plateau, the 245- to 570-million-year-old Paleozoic rocks are buried. Little would be known about the inland oceans and stream-laced plains that covered Utah during that time if the rivers had not carved canyons throughout it, revealing the deepest layers of time. Drill bits used by the oil-and-gas industry have offered many clues, too, as have the major uplifts of land that brought older rocks up to eye level. But the canyons are our main windows to Paleozoic time, when amphibians first crawled onto the land.

To see and touch the oldest of these rocks, you have to raft down one of the rivers that slice through canyon country—the Colorado, San Juan, and Green are almost everyone's favorites. The Colorado River's Grand Canyon and Westwater Canyon exhibit rocks even older than Paleozoic time, but we chose to raft through Cataract Canyon on the Colorado. Our trip plunged us into the heart of Canyonlands National Park one hot July, as the temperature topped 105 degrees.

"Plunge" may not be the right word (though most folks who venture through Cataract's rapids feel like they have taken the plunge of their lives), because we spilled into Cataract when the river level was at an all-time low. Low water made the rapids less wild and the trip more tranquil. But this allowed us to focus on the rock layers above us, the sandbars beneath, and the bighorn sheep coming out of the bone-dry canyon for a sip of warm, mud-flavored water.

Ironically, some of the darkest reaches of early geologic history in canyon country are the most bleached out. The oldest rock we saw was a chalky jumble belonging to what is called the Paradox formation. We spotted it the first time at Spanish Bottom. As we rounded a bend, it seemed to jump out at us, a messy blob of what our boatman called "that squished-up, grungy, white crud." He said it was a plug of gypsum that had pushed its way up to the surface from beds of the Paradox formation hundreds of feet down.

This chalky plug of Paradox seemed aptly named. Not only was it a crazy anomaly out of nowhere, but this bleached-out lump, the oldest visible thing in what is now a desert-like land, was also formed under the wettest of environments—a sea. Not just one sea but twenty-nine—or actually, twenty-nine "cycles" of sea water, which flowed in when the level of the mother ocean was high and retreated when that level dropped. Furthermore, these twenty-nine sea cycles existed in a very hot, arid environment in which water evaporated quickly.

The main feature of the landscape during Pennsylvanian time was the Uncompahgre Uplift, a long, ridge-like highland. Alongside and parallel to it was a giant bowl, the Paradox Basin. Both features lay along an ancient basement fault that formed during Precambrian time, before the Paleozoic era.

PERIOD	PENNSYLVANIAN *(286–320 MILLION YEARS AGO)*	PERMIAN *(245–286 MILLION YEARS AGO)*	TRIASSIC *(208–245 MILLION YEARS AGO)*	
ERA	PALEOZOIC			

The twenty-nine seas story starts in the middle of the Pennsylvanian period, about three hundred million years ago. About that time, a major highland, called the Uncompahgre Uplift, rose up along an ancient fault, while a huge basin about the size of West Virginia sank down along its southwest side. Sea water rushed in from the west and south and rapidly filled the basin. Soon the sea stagnated and left behind a crusty residue of gypsum, salt, and carbonates from the evaporation of the marine water. The sea repeated this exercise, advancing and retreating, twenty-nine times. Each time it laid down another crusty layer until thousands of feet of salts and other evaporites had built up in the basin, creating the Paradox formation.

The bottom of the basin continued to sink, deepening the depression and ultimately resulting in an oval-shaped bowl some two hundred miles long. Years later, the salt in the Paradox Basin would be buried by tons of other sediments piling on top of it. In fact, the weight of these later sediments would become so heavy that the buoyant salt would start to "flow" away from the pressure. Wherever it could find a weak spot, the salt would punch through the surface, like toothpaste bursting through a pinhole in the tube. This is how our salty blob of gypsum, called Prommel Dome, was able to peek its dirty white head out, hundreds of feet above its original bed. Although Paradox rocks are over three hundred million years old, you can still taste the salt of the sea in them.

The morning after we passed Spanish Bottom and Prommel Dome, the water was placid, the scene timeless, as we drifted out into the current and began floating downstream. Then suddenly, the sound of roiling water jarred our daydreaming. Before we knew it, we had lost sight of the Paradox and were moving very fast into the pools above Cataract Canyon's Rapid #1. With little warning, we went from the calm into the eye of the storm, scraping bottom on submerged rocks hidden in the chutes. One of these boulders tipped our raft up nearly vertical for a moment until we spun loose. We realized that even at lowest water, Cataract demands attention. Another twenty-seven rapids still lay ahead. The geohistory of the canyon would have to take a backseat for a while.

CANYON COUNTRY IN PENNSYLVANIAN TIME (ABOUT 300 MILLION YEARS AGO)

The section of geologic time below shows just the geologic eras and periods that cover the canyon country rocks. Paleozoic time is marked by the appearance of the first fish, reptiles, and reptile-like mammals. The Mesozoic was the age of the dinosaurs, and the Cenozoic, the age of mammals. If human existence were marked on this scale, it would amount to about one sixteenth of an inch.

JURASSIC (144–208 MILLION YEARS AGO)	CRETACEOUS (66.4–144 MILLION YEARS AGO)	TERTIARY (1.6–66.4 MILLION YEARS AGO)	QUATERNARY (0–1.6 MILLION YEARS AGO)
MESOZOIC		CENOZOIC	

Lake Powell—
created when a man-
made dam on the
Colorado River flooded
Glen Canyon—is
ironically named for
John Wesley Powell, a
man who was among
the first to raft down the
uncharted wild waters
of Cataract Canyon, the
rough-water section
upstream from Glen
Canyon.

Once we were past the first few rapids, we stopped for a break on a sandbar, taking our focus off the rushing water for a bit. Looking up, we could see the strata just above the Paradox. It was a drab, gray, stairstep affair that the guidebooks listed as the Honaker Trail formation, left behind when the sea finally returned in late Pennsylvanian time, some 290 million years ago. Before we floated the river, we had seen the Honaker Trail formation at the entrenched meanders of the San Juan River called the Goosenecks. There, it was a masterpiece of symmetry—perfect stairsteps of parallel limestone and sandstone ledges, separated by shale slopes. But here on the river it didn't seem so symmetrical. It was contorted, roughed up. The Paradox, apparently, was the culprit: the bulging salt had bent and deformed the Honaker Trail so much that we hardly recognized it. This was not the last time we were to see Utah's landscape twisted, bulged, or arched up due to the buoyant Paradox trying to ooze its way to the top.

* * *

After rocking and rumbling through the last rapid, we leaned back and just floated. The river was placid again, the way it had been before the rapids, but the difference in canyon color downstream versus upstream was striking. The drab grays, pale browns, and dirty whites that engulfed us after crashing through the rough water contrasted vividly with the color we had seen earlier, upstream.

Before the rapids and upriver from Spanish Bottom and Prommel Dome, our little flotilla had been engulfed in brilliant maroons, purples, and deep reds. It was as if we had been dunked in a bath of wine as we floated past ruby- and burgundy-colored siltstones and mudstones, all rounded and smooth like rouge-painted cheeks. That was when we were passing through what's known as the Cutler formation, a remnant of iron-rich sediments that washed down from the Uncompahgre Uplift. Why so much red? When iron-bearing minerals decompose, they literally rust, producing all the hues in the red spectrum—purple, wine, orange, cardinal, maroon, magenta, scarlet, cochineal. The Cutler formation sits above the Honaker Trail formation and dominates the next chapter in this geologic story, the Permian period, which started about 290 million years ago.

The Cutler formation is complex and sometimes confuses even the experts. It was set down amid a maze of different landscapes, which included coastal environments as well as freshwater streams and dune fields. At the edge of the sea, there was a mix of beach sands, sandbars, and tidal mudflats. But the sea levels fluctuated a lot, so shorelines were constantly shifting, and beaches moved around. Coastal plains and lagoons were found not far from the water. Away from the shoreline, windblown sand dunes accumulated up on higher ground, where the freshwater streams flowed, hauling tons of red sediment down from the highlands of the Uncompahgre. These landscapes are preserved today in the layers known as Halgaito shale, Cedar Mesa sandstone, Organ Rock shale, De Chelly sandstone, White Rim sandstone, and Lower Cutler (also called Elephant Canyon formation)—all of which make up the Cutler Group.

To make matters worse, during Cutler time the old Paradox salt was still on the move. It continued to cause bulges in the topography, creating mountains out of molehills and generally causing consternation for the streams flowing down out of the Uncompahgre high country.

Near Spanish Bottom, before the rapids, we saw the Cedar Mesa sandstone—the most famous rock star of the Cutler group. Dancing above the canyon walls were the candy-striped pinnacles of the Doll House, a crazy, sculpted collection of "dolls" hewn out of Cedar Mesa sandstone. Cedar Mesa is also the mother stone of similarly banded spires on the other side of the river, called the Needles.

"Why the red and white bands?" one of the raft passengers asked, studying the carmine and cream pinnacles. The answer focused on the complex geography and hydrology that characterized Cutler time. While red sediments were being deposited by streams from the northeast, white sand was arriving simultaneously from the northwest, carried either by water or wind. The red sediments interfingered with the whites, forming alternating bands of color. The venue for this red-and-white rendezvous was exactly where the Needles and the Doll House exist today. The red sediment beds petered out to the southwest as they got farther away from their iron-rich mother mountain, the old Uncompahgre Uplift. Because of sheer distance from the Uncompahgre, Cedar Mesa sandstone west and south of Canyonlands is almost pure white. Witness the bridges of vanilla-colored stone in Natural Bridges National Monument.

The Cutler was the last exposed layer of Paleozoic strata we saw on the river. But it is not the final layer of the Paleozoic (or of the Permian period) existing in southeastern Utah. There is one more.

Small outcrops of a modest marine deposit—the Kaibab formation, dating back 255 million years—can be seen in Capitol Reef National Park and on the San Rafael Swell. (Kaibab is also the rimrock of the Grand Canyon.) Largely a limey sediment called dolomite, the Kaibab is a leftover from the last Permian sea, which lay mostly to the west of our area. That sea only lightly lapped at the edges of canyon country. The Kaibab is the calling card it left behind.

* * *

By the time the Kaibab was forming at the end of the Paleozoic era, the once mighty Uncompahgre Uplift had worn down considerably. It was now much lower than it had been in Paradox days. Since this northeastern highland had been the primary source of the iron-rich sediments, this was also the finale of the red beds that characterize Canyonlands.

The Paleozoic era seemed to end quietly, as did our river trip, as we approached the take-out point of Hite, and the placid waters of Lake Powell drifted us slowly to the marina.

Deserts, Plains, and the Last Great Sea: The Mesozoic Era

With the close of the Paleozoic era, thus ended all those other troublesome P's—Pennsylvanian, Permian, and Paradox. As we grappled to keep track of all the strata we had seen, we remembered geologist Michael Collier's headaches taking a similar tally of rock types

The Goosenecks of
the San Juan River are
classic examples of
entrenched river mean-
ders—deeply incised,
loop-around canyons.
As the San Juan, a
major tributary of the
Colorado River, became
inescapably entrapped
in its own erosional
channel, it left behind
stairsteplike ledges
in the Honaker Trail
formation.

Monument Valley (below) is one of the best places to see the spires and cliffs of De Chelly sandstone and its sloping skirts of Organ Rock shale.

The Moenkopi formation (left) is a chocolate-red silty mudstone that forms either convoluted sculptured cliffs like these in the Capitol Reef area or slopes and ledges in the eastern part of canyon country.

A mudstone called Hoodoo Entrada (left) can be seen in the western part of canyon country.

Cedar Mesa sandstone in Canyonlands National Park is a candy cane sculpture of red-and-white-banded rock—the result of red sediments interfingering with white sediments some 290 million years ago.

Navajo sandstone, pictured here in Capitol Reef National Park, was formed from sand dunes and is widely found in the Southwest.

such as oceans, dune fields, lagoons, or wandering streams.

The rock sculptures and pinnacles found throughout canyon country were hewn by the forces of erosion. Harder layers of rock are more resistant to erosion and remain in place, while the softer layers of rock are gradually eaten away by wind and water. Canyon country was created by this process, called "differential erosion."

The hardest layers of rock tend to be the limestones and sandstones that form cliffs, spires, buttes, benches, pinnacles, and overhangs. The softer shales and siltstones form rounded hills and gentle slopes of loose materials. The vertical cliffs of the canyon country, for example, often have soft, gentle slopes below them, like the Wingate sandstone and its skirt of Chinle shale.

Wingate sandstone (right) dominates the horizon over much of southeast Utah and can be recognized at a distance by its sheer, dark, stockadelike line of cliffs. Wingate walls are frequently coated with desert varnish.

GEOLOGY OF THE LAND OF CANYONS

A great variety of events, millions of years ago, created the bare rocks of the canyon country landscape. When sand dunes were piling up in one area of today's slickrock wildlands, ocean waves were lapping across another. Streams hauled in sediments near silty mudflats. White sediments accumulated in one place, while red beds dominated in another. Volcanic ash clouded the skies and blanketed everything in one part of the region, while other places were too far from the volcanoes to be dusted with any airborne ash. These different "depositional environments" created the unique geological character of canyon country.

Over time, the various sediments that were laid down hardened and consolidated into rock. The layers of rock, or "formations," as they are called, stack up in the order in which they were laid down. The differences in their color and texture reflect the different conditions that existed when they were formed—

GEOLOGIC PROFILES OF ROCK LAYERS

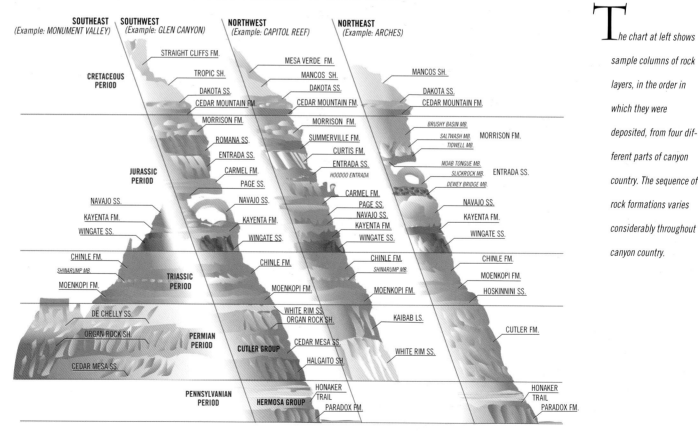

FM. = Formation., SS. = Sandstone., SH. = Shale., LM. = Limestone., MB. = Member.

The chart at left shows sample columns of rock layers, in the order in which they were deposited, from four different parts of canyon country. The sequence of rock formations varies considerably throughout canyon country.

The Chinle formation (left) is well known for its uranium and the slipperiness of its roads. Deposited by streams, it is easy to recognize as the pastel-colored skirt under the sheer cliffs of Wingate sandstone.

The slickrock member of the Entrada sandstone (below) was formed from dunes. It is best known for its mono-liths and natural arches in the area around Moab, Utah.

The Summerville formation (left) forms crumbly cliffs in a side canyon of the Fremont River.

The Morrison formation (above) is a slope-forming shale of mauve, turquoise, and pink hues, frequently littered with boulders of Dakota sandstone.

the landscape, and these events varied also in strength, locale, and type. This is why through-out canyon country there are mountains in some places, valleys in others, and varied deforma-tions of the surface crust—faults, ripples, and folds—in between.

The Canyonlands section of the Colorado Plateau—what we know as canyon country—is a place that no one can forget once they have seen it. Its brilliant colors, striking formations, and bare expanses of slickrock are products of a complex geological past undupli-cated anywhere in the world.

The gray and dull gold col-ors of Mancos shale (right) cover a huge expanse of canyon country and contrast sharply with the brilliant reds, ivories, and yellows of the sandstones.

Differences in depositional environments combined with differential erosion explain much of the variety in the canyon country landscape today—but not all. Tectonic forces later bent, heaved up, tore down, and in other ways deformed

The La Sal Mountains
tower in the distance over
Water Canyon in
Canyonlands National
Park, on the west side of
the Colorado River.

in Capitol Reef National Park. Trying to sort out one rock layer from another on a hike to Brimhall Bridge, he finally pleads, "No more sedimentary strata . . . . No more limey sandstones and sandy limestones." Like us, he had reached the point where he wanted to let go of the names, lists, and geological descriptions and just sit back and enjoy it all.

Ready to do that, too, we returned to Moab, arriving at Grand View Point on the Island in the Sky in Canyonlands National Park just in time for sunset. It was a grand view indeed. What looked like the entire canyon country stretched out in front of us from our vantage point on the edge of a four-hundred-foot-high cliff.

The stack of chocolate-brown rocks we stood on were laid down during the Triassic period, a fairly peaceful time on the not-yet-born Colorado Plateau. When the Triassic opened, 245 million years ago, an ocean still covered much of the West. Large reptiles roamed the higher ground, which was covered with arid plains and jungle-like tangles along the streams. The last Permian sea had retreated into what is now western Utah, but its intertidal mudflats stretched for hundreds of miles to the east. Streams flowed into the tidal mudflats from present-day Arizona and Colorado, bringing in fine-grained silt. Tidal currents helped to swish around and distribute the stream silt, spreading out thin coatings of the silt and mud. Dark laminations of the sediments began to accumulate, creating the cocoa-colored mudstone called the Moenkopi formation. Its origin in shallow waters is obvious when you see the ripple marks preserved in slabs of Moenkopi rock.

Thicker stacks of mud and silt laminations built up closer to the sea, so when we first met the Moenkopi at Capitol Reef National Park on the western fringes of canyon country, it was a thirty-foot-high, convoluted, mudstone cliff, colored and layered like a chocolate torte. It seemed so different from the other strata that we thought we would always recognize it.

However, the Moenkopi tricked us. It thins considerably as it reaches eastward, and from Grand View Point in the sunset light, it no longer looked like a torte. It was more of a ledge-slope-ledge affair, punctuated by squatty cliffs, and it had changed in color from chocolate to cherry-brown. (Maybe every formation blushes when it gets close to Canyonlands.) The change in color from brown to red is probably due to more red pigment showing up the closer we came to the source of the streams that carried the silt.

Eventually, the sea that had splashed around the Moenkopi muds retreated even farther west. And the streams dried up that had carried the silt into the intertidal zone. Now the Moenkopi mudflats "were left high and dry to bake in the hot sun for perhaps ten million years," as geologist Don Baars describes the Triassic oven that followed.

* * *

If we had been prospecting for uranium, the slopes just above the Moenkopi would have been a good place to look—the Chinle formation. Its shades of pale blue, baby pink, gray, faint turquoise, green, and lavender tinted the slopes below our four-hundred-foot

A view of some of prominent geologic formations in canyon country from Sulphur Creek in Capitol Reef National Park. Navajo sandstone forms the high cliffs in the background. Below the Navajo (in order) are layers of the Kayenta formation, Wingate sandstone, Chinle formation, and Moenkopi formation.

cliff. The hues of pink and lavender were produced when iron in the sediments was exposed to air, while the blues and greens were formed in stagnant water without oxygen. The Chinle formation created a shale petticoat of pastels that flounced out from the base of the cliff we stood on.

Wanting to look closer at the Chinle, we wondered if we could hike down to it—a drop of four hundred feet or so. According to the map, there was a route—the Gooseberry Trail—leading over the edge and down the cliff, through a place where a landslide and a series of ledges allowed passage.

The next morning we gave it a try. We switchbacked down the steep cliff face to the pastel slopes, then slid through the loose shale until we finally skidded to a stop at a light brown ledge. The ledge was a rough-textured conglomerate of sands and gravels left from streams that had meandered across the cracked and dried Moenkopi mudflats. These streams carried a mix of sediments and plant debris: the recipe for uranium ore. The plant material had acted as a catalyst in the precipitation of uranium minerals. As a result, this modest ledge, rich in fossil plants, was the hope chest of many prospectors who dreamed of a fortune in uranium. Hundreds of such dreamers were drawn to southeast Utah during the "atomic age" uranium boom that put Moab on the map in the 1950s. Fossil plants also show up in the Chinle as petrified wood.

While the Chinle sediments were being deposited, fine-grained ash was settling over everything, dusting the landscape like a dirty gray snow. Ash filtered down from volcanic eruptions outside canyon country, probably to the southwest. This is the stuff that bentonite clay comes from, and it is bentonite that makes the roads slippery when they're wet. Anyone who has lived in the canyon country for long knows the deeper meaning behind the "Slippery When Wet" signs on dirt roads. The signs that say "Impassable When Wet" are more honest. Bentonite is the devil in a clay bubble. Best to just avoid the Chinle in a rainstorm.

* * *

On our ascent back up the Gooseberry Trail, we talked about how rare it is to find walkable routes anywhere through cliffs like the one in front of us. The dark brown, sheer wall seemed to form an almost impenetrable rock barrier that extended horizontally in both directions as far as our eyes could see. It encircled all the land below it, truly forming an island in the sky. This was the Wingate sandstone, the bodice above the Chinle petticoat and the first of the great sandstones of the Jurassic period.

Although there has been considerable debate about exactly when the Triassic period ended and the Jurassic period began, it is certain that at some point, the climate began to change, becoming so hot and dry that the Chinle streams dried up. The wind began to blow. Sand pelted everything in sight and settled into drifts, first building up the great dunes that would eventually become the Wingate sandstone, then stockpiling almost pure quartz that would harden into ivory-colored Navajo sandstone and Page sandstone, and later building up piles that would become known as Entrada sandstone. The Entrada varied somewhat across the

The Chinle formation, largely comprised of shale, forms gentle slopes which erode into soft, rounded profiles. Sandstones, on the other hand, form massive blocks that weather into cliffs, domes, and buttresses.

FOLLOWING PAGES:

Navajo sandstone, widespread across the Colorado Plateau, forms prominent domes and walls in the Escalante watershed, pictured here, as well as the great cliffs in Zion National Park. Its light color contrasts with the dark green of the pinyon and juniper trees that grow in its cracks and sandy pockets.

The graceful Temple of the Moon, carved from the silty Hoodoo Entrada sandstone, is located in Cathedral Valley in Capitol Reef National Park. The same formation produced mushroom, goblin, and dwarf shapes that enchanted poet Walt Whitman and which are best seen in Goblin Valley State Park.

region: to the west, it was dampened by wetlands, but eastward near the water's edge, beach dunes built up. These beach sands resulted in the tawny-colored rock called the slickrock member of the Entrada, well known today for its arches, so prominent around Moab. Where Entrada's beach sands gave way to the muddy silts of the wetlands, a silty version was created, called Hoodoo Entrada by locals in the western part of canyon country for the russet-colored goblin, elf, and mushroom shapes in the fantasy land of Goblin Valley.

We wanted to immerse ourselves in the Jurassic desert days, so we left Grand View Point and headed for Arches National Park. It wasn't hard to imagine what it was like back in the super-hot Jurassic period, because the temperature peaked at 113 degrees the day we went out to walk amid wall-like fins, arches, slickrock benches, and balanced rocks. Hot blasts of wind tore our hats off as we stood staring up at the monoliths at Park Avenue. Had dinosaurs worn hats in Jurassic days, this would have happened to them, too. But they did have brief respites from the wind and sand. The Jurassic desert dune environment was interrupted three times for relatively short periods during which streams or seas calmed the swirling sands, although the climate remained hot and dry.

The first of these interruptions came at the end of the Wingate desert and left behind the stream-deposited Kayenta formation, right on top of the Wingate's desert dunes. In *Canyoneering*, Steve Allen says that the Kayenta, which weathers into rounded lips, is the favorite route for hikers because of its flat, walkable ledges. Kayenta was also a preferred path for prehistoric walkers such as dinosaurs, whose footprints are preserved in what was once wet sand and muddy silt.

The second time streams threaded their way through the dunes, the formation immediately above the Navajo and Page sandstones was created. This rock layer is called the Carmel formation to the west and Dewey Bridge to the east—although geologists actually consider the crinkled, brick-red Dewey Bridge to be a "member" of the Entrada sandstone.

Unlike the first two interruptions, which cast fresh water over the sands, the third and last wetting of the dune field brought the return of the sea, which had been waiting patiently in the wings to the north. It reached southward and dampened the Entrada silts and sands in just a little corner of canyon country. White marine sandstone resulted, known as the Curtis formation in the San Rafael/Capitol Reef area. At the same time, a white, windblown sandstone called the Moab Tongue of the Entrada was forming in the east on top of its older cousin, Entrada's slickrock member.

When the Curtis sea retreated, it left behind mudflats where its deep waters had been, and as in the Moenkopi days, laminations of silt stacked up. These thin, silty layers would eventually became the dull brown Summerville formation, which lies just above the Curtis in the west and interfingers with the Moab Tongue to the east. To the southwest, the Romana sandstone, a sandier layer, replaced the Summerville.

If you don't count its three brief "dampening" episodes—collectively amounting to a few million years of streams or seas—the Jurassic "Sahara" desert of dunes lasted one helluva long time, even by geological standards: almost fifty million years. It was as widespread as it was long-lived. Its broadest sweep occurred when the Navajo sandstone desert buried everything from Colorado to Nevada and from Arizona to Wyoming in ivory-colored sand. Today it is noted as the greatest dune field ever recorded in North America—possibly the greatest ever recorded anywhere!

Still holding on to our hats and reeling a bit from the heat, we felt as if we had been there—in Jurassic Park, or Jurassic Desert National Park, one hundred fifty million years ago.

* * *

We drove out of Arches National Park toward the northwest. After about twenty minutes, we saw ahead of us some low, rounded hills of pale turquoise and mauve—the Morrison formation—a striking contrast to the massive, red sandstone fins and cliffs that surrounded us in Arches. There was not one plant growing on the Morrison hills. As we climbed up the greenish-blue "popcorn" slopes (and tried sliding down, only to discover—to the discomfort of our elbows and rear ends—that the Morrison isn't very slidable), it seemed that we had experienced this scene before. The lakes and streams that produced the dinosaur haven called the Morrison directly followed the silty Summerville mudslicks and the Moab Tongue dunes, so this had to be a new layer for us. Was this a geological deja vu? Then, suddenly, we realized why the Morrison looked so familiar. The Chinle, the pastel petticoat! Morrison is a dead-ringer for the Chinle—same blue-greens and pinks, similar lake and stream origins, same old devil bentonite clay and equivalent uranium. But the Morrison is much younger—in fact, it was our last Jurassic experience.

Above the Morrison's popcorn slopes, where we had slid, was a little brown cliff of broken pieces, the Dakota sandstone. We stood on the Dakota ledge and looked down, noticing that many Dakota sandstone boulders had broken off and were littering the turquoise skirts below. Most people would never even notice this inconspicuous brown ledge, since neither its color nor its shape is notable.

But the Dakota marks an important moment in Utah's geologic history: as the shoreline frontrunner of an advancing sea, it signals the return of marine conditions for the last and final time in canyon country. (That is, until the San Andreas Fault in California pops the big one and creates beachfront property in Bluff and Hanksville.) Except for a few lake and stream deposits (the Cedar Mountain formation, for example) that preceded it, the Dakota also marks the beginning of a new period, the Cretaceous.

Not particularly enchanted with the Dakota (but nonetheless impressed with its benchmark status), we drove a few miles farther north. This put some distance between us and the red rocks of Arches.

This side canyon in the Escalante watershed flows almost year-round. It has cut its way down through the resistant Kayenta formation, a rock type well known as a likely place to find dinosaur bones and tracks.

We stopped just beyond the Greater Moab International Airport. A strong wind scattered our papers and blew the door shut on the truck. We tried to get our eyes to focus on a whole new set of colors—the grays, charcoals, and brownish golds of the Mancos shale. For several minutes we stared blankly at the desolate, low hills of Mancos in front of us. Missing were the vibrant reds and the stunning cliffs of other parts of canyon country. With muted colors and shaley hills in lieu of solid rock, this was indeed a very different scene.

The Mancos—which blankets a huge expanse of canyon country—and a parallel formation that occurs farther south, Tropic shale, were formed when the Cretaceous sea deepened and thick, black mud settled to the bottom. Organic debris, too, got tangled up in the dark slimy ooze. Stinky and stagnant, this oxygen-deprived environment was the dark cradle where the Mancos and Tropic shales were born.

Ebbing and flowing like most oceans, the last canyon country sea advanced several times during its life span. Its hopscotch movement across the continent created successive shorelines that are today recorded in the sandstone cliffs of the Mesaverde Group and the Straight Cliffs formation. Wanting to be closer to the cliffs while we explored the Mancos, we drove another twenty minutes north, then took a walk into the gray mounds where the buff-colored Book Cliffs of the Mesaverde Group towered above the Mancos. Our feet crunched the hardened crust of the shale. Everything around us was gray, including three prairie dogs that scuttled in front of our feet and several lizards that zipped past. Even the plants were gray, as if something other than chlorophyll had taken over photosynthesis. Mat saltbush dominated, a prostrate, ashen, vegetative doily thriving on soil that would destroy most plants. This scene was as faded and as drained of color as any we had ever seen. It was rivaled only by the bleakness of the Tropic shale and the Straight Cliffs we visited near Lake Powell.

So now we had come full circle. After starting out on the river in the drab Paradox and Honaker Trail formations of the Pennsylvanian period, we had returned to similarly drab grays at the close of the Cretaceous period, some two hundred million years later, which also ended the Mesozoic era. However, the dull grays of limestone, shale, sage, shadscale, and saltbush served as modest counterpoints to all those fierce and flagrant crimsons—like an unassuming farmboy in faded jeans escorting a beauty queen in a carmine gown. Without the grays of canyon country, the reds would be less vibrant. Without the subdued mounds of the Mancos, the towering cliffs of Entrada would not be so towering. All of the hues—red, purple, blue, green, and gray—add to the rainbow palette that colors the incredible variety of shapes—arches, cliffs, slopes, as well as small, inconspicuous ridges. It's all part of the geological parfait. All part of the sedimentary saga.

Not all of south-
east Utah is red, nor is
it all rock. On plateaus
and between canyons
are commonly found
open plains like the
Burr Desert,
pictured here, near the
Dirty Devil River.

A cool wind whipped the flames of our little five-inch campfire, where red-hot coals were glowing wild in the Zipstove. An early summer storm was coming. It may have been too soon in the season to worry about floods, but it's hard to predict which storms will have rain heavy enough to make the washes run, and we were glad we had gotten across several drainages before the storm hit. Our campsite was nestled below an overhang in the San Rafael Swell country.

* * *

Gary remembers: Once I missed a whopper of a flash flood by just one day. I had kayaked up Lake Powell to Dark Canyon right after a flood had left a ten-foot-tall tongue of red mud, rotting leaf litter, dead cows, and splintered cottonwood trunks at the mouth of the canyon. The stench was strong: the muskiness of the wet soil and composting leaf, the decay of dead, half-buried animals. It took nearly an hour to maneuver the first half mile past this delta of newly accumulated debris. As I climbed over, around, and through its tunnels encased in flotsam, I felt grateful I had not arrived the day before, when that frothing, seething mass was still moving.

* * *

Caroline remembers: In Ed Abbey's account of a flash flood in *Slickrock*, he describes his car being stuck in the middle of North Wash, and he can't figure out what his friends are frantically yelling at him from upstream: "Mud?" "Blood?" "Crud?"

A tributary in Glen Canyon National Recreation Area.

WHERE WATER RULES

SCULPTING ARCH, BRIDGE, AND CLIFF

He barely realizes in time that they are screaming, "FLOOD!"

My family and I were almost swept away in a similar flash flood in North Wash when I was about six or seven. We'd gone down to Natural Bridges from Moab, in the old government Chevrolet coupe.

It was a clear August day when we started back, crossing on the ferry at Hite, then heading up North Wash. All of a sudden, my mother leaned her head out the window. "What's that noise? Sounds like thunder," she said. My dad stuck his head out the window, then muttered, "Oh, my God!" Without another word, he jerked the steering wheel to the left, stepped on the gas, and whipped the car right over a small shrub and up onto the nearest bank above the wash.

We all tumbled out of the black Chevrolet and stared. No more than twenty yards upstream, there came a froth of foam and flotsam that was the color and consistency of a chocolate milkshake.

I had never seen anything like it. A ton of muddy water was right behind that foam. What my mother had heard was the roar of the flood, which we heard, too, before we could see it. Within minutes, the shrub we had driven over was drowned in three feet of water. Incredibly fast.

We were stuck there for the night. The flood picked up trees and rocks and swept them downstream, scouring the canyon with a great force. The roar was like a busy freeway, and the ground shook beneath us all night long.

The flood could have taken us, too, burying us in a mountain of flotsam like those drowned cows Gary saw at the mouth of Dark Canyon.

* * *

Anyone witnessing a flash flood in this country has reason to be humbled by its sheer force and nondiscriminating power. Water—that rare desert noun—has been the single most pervasive verb in canyon country vocabulary. Water has played a key role here over the last three hundred million years, hauling in more than half of the sediments that make up the rock layers. But the role of water in deposition is small when compared to its role as the carver, the eater, the agent in charge of tearing up the landscape. And once the layer cake of canyon country was more or less complete, with all its strata in place (which it was by the end of the Cretaceous period), there was nothing left to do but start tearing it down.

The first step in this process—before water and other weathering agents could get in to do their work—was the creation of cracks, buckles, folds, tilts, mountains, and other deformations in the surface of the landscape.

For starters, at the beginning of the Tertiary period, about sixty-five million years ago, the canyon country was hit with what many geologists feel was the most gut-wrenching event ever in its geohistory. A great continental wave of compression, the Laramide

The major folding and faulting of the earth's crust during early to middle Tertiary time molded the landscape into the major surface features—the basins, uplifts, and mountains—we see today in canyon country.

Orogeny, rippled across the West, creating buckles in the earth's crust. This wave of compression elevated the great uplifts and folded the monstrous monoclines of today's landscape into their present-day profiles.

　　After the Laramide dust had settled, molten rock was quietly brewing below the earth's surface at several spots in canyon country. Beginning in mid-Tertiary time, about twenty-five to thirty million years ago, the magma began pushing upwards, creating igneous intrusions, arching strata above, and creating major bumps on the horizon—the Henry, La Sal, and Abajo Mountains. Navajo Mountain was probably created in this way, too, but because its inner core is still well concealed, we won't know for sure about its origin until erosion strips it down.

**CANYON COUNTRY IN TERTIARY TIME
(15 MILLION YEARS AGO)**

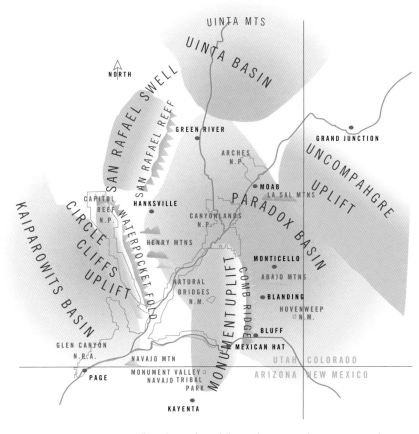

　　Meanwhile, the whole region was tilted like a teeter-totter to the north. That is, the south end of canyon country went up, and the north end dipped down. Erosion escalated with the new tilt. And as if that were not enough, between fifteen and twenty-five million years ago, the entire Colorado Plateau began to rise, slowly pushing upward until it had come up several thousand feet, finally earning its name as a plateau.

　　The upshot of all this action was that the layer cake of canyon country lost its level-headed outlook on life. The elevation of the plateau was particularly devastating. With that uprising, drainage gradients steepened. Erosion accelerated. In contrast to the years of quiet deposition, the pedal was now pressed hard to the floorboard—although in geologic time, this means only a few inches of erosion every couple of hundred years.

　　For the next fifteen million years, the mischief of wind and water reached into every crack and crevice. From this point forward in this geologic story, erosion, rather than deposition, ruled. The deepest canyons in canyon country were carved in the last five million years, and most of the landscape we see today was molded into its basic form in just the last 1.6 million years.

*　*　*

SLICKROCK CARVINGS

Canyon country contains some of the most spectacular natural architecture in the world, created by the process of erosion. A mesa is a flat-topped plateau, named after the Spanish word for table. A butte is a plateau that has eroded to a shape that is as wide as it is tall. A spire, on the other hand, is a butte that has weathered into a column that is taller than it is wide.

Other unique forms, such as natural arches and bridges, are found throughout the canyon country landscape. An arch is a hole or window in rock formed by the combined action of frost, wind, and water,

while bridges are created by the carving action of water running through a drainage. Natural Bridges National Monument contains some of the finest examples in the world, carved in Cedar Mesa sandstone. Rainbow Bridge, a massive arc of Navajo sandstone, is one of the world's best-known natural bridges.

The buttes and pinnacles of Monument Valley are eroded remnants of De Chelly sandstone.

Water is only sporadically seen going about its work, as we saw with the flash flood. Other forces are even less apparent—the secret agents of erosion. When aided by the wedging action of ice and plant roots, wind is the quiet archbishop, giving its final blessings on the holes, alcoves, windows, and arches that water creates. Wind also sculpts. It goes directly for the soft spots, like looser-grained pockets of sandstone that are vulnerable to the abrasive power of swirling grains of sand. It is always busy rounding, routing, polishing, and sanding. Sometimes it seems as if wind were made to live side by side with sandstone.

But water is the master carver, the canyon cutter, and the scouring pad of this country. Running water—whether it be the largest flash flood or the tiniest trickle—has done more to create the canyon country topography than any other force. Water is not quite as secretive about its work as wind; we are more likely to see and hear it in action. Even if you get to witness water at work, it is easy to forget that most of this landscape has been shaped by the ten days a year when rain is heavy and the washes run hard. Rare events, not the day to day, mold the canyon country.

Water in all its forms—ice, trickles, snow, mist, and floods—takes its toll on the land. When it freezes, it expands and wedges little cracks into bigger ones. When, in any form, it contacts rock, shale, sand, or any other type of substrate, water hastens the process of erosion by initiating the dissolution of the cement that holds the sediment grains together. When water flows, it sweeps away whatever is in its path that it has the power to lift. That might be just the uppermost fraction of an inch of sandy crust on a cliff face or five feet of fill in the bottom of a wash. It isn't so much the flowing water itself that wreaks havoc as what it carries. From the abrasion of wet grit trickling down a slickrock cliff face to the slurry of gravel and boulders crashing in a flood, the material carried by flowing water is what scoured channels below bridges, carved cliffs, formed meanders, and sliced canyons, cutting out the maze of geological vertebrae that form the skeleton of southeast Utah. This dry land could never have been called "canyon country" without water.

Take away the knifelike actions of wind and water cutting through the layer cake, and the Colorado Plateau might have turned out more like the Great Plains—with gently sloping edges, its borders blurred. Instead, we have goosenecks, oxbows, fins, needles, spires, joints, alcoves, overhangs, mesas, grabens, buttes, bridges, arches, windows, plateaus . . . topography of unspeakable complexity.

FOLLOWING PAGES:

*N*ear Muley Point, the setting sun casts peach and lavender hues on the stairstep ledges of Cedar Mesa sandstone. Cedar Mesa is also the rock of the Doll House and the Needles in Canyonlands National Park, as well as the bridges in Natural Bridges National Monument.

WINDOWS IN STONE

Thin fins of sandstone, like these at left in Arches National Park, are likely places for natural arches to form. The thinner the fin, the more vulnerable it is to erosion.

Most natural arches in southeast Utah are carved in Entrada and Navajo sandstone. The arch-forming process begins when carbon dioxide in rainwater dissolves the cement that holds the stone's grains of sand together, allowing the loosened grains to be easily blown or washed away. The tiny hole or crack left behind then widens when winter comes and water seeps in, freezes, and expands. Once a hole gets started in the sandstone, pieces of rock tend to fall off from the top of the opening. In this way, a very small hole can gradually grow to form a window or an arch.

*C*lear, perennial waterfalls, like Lower Calf Creek Falls in the Escalante, are rare sights in canyon country and are often tucked away in the depths of hidden canyons. More commonly seen are chocolate-colored cascades streaming down rock faces during times of flood.

*S*lot canyons are the thinnest of abysses. Between their vertical walls, often only an armspan apart, can be a void that may plummet to a depth of fifty feet or more.

Slot canyons are usually carved through rock of uniform hardness by watercourses which have nowhere else to go.

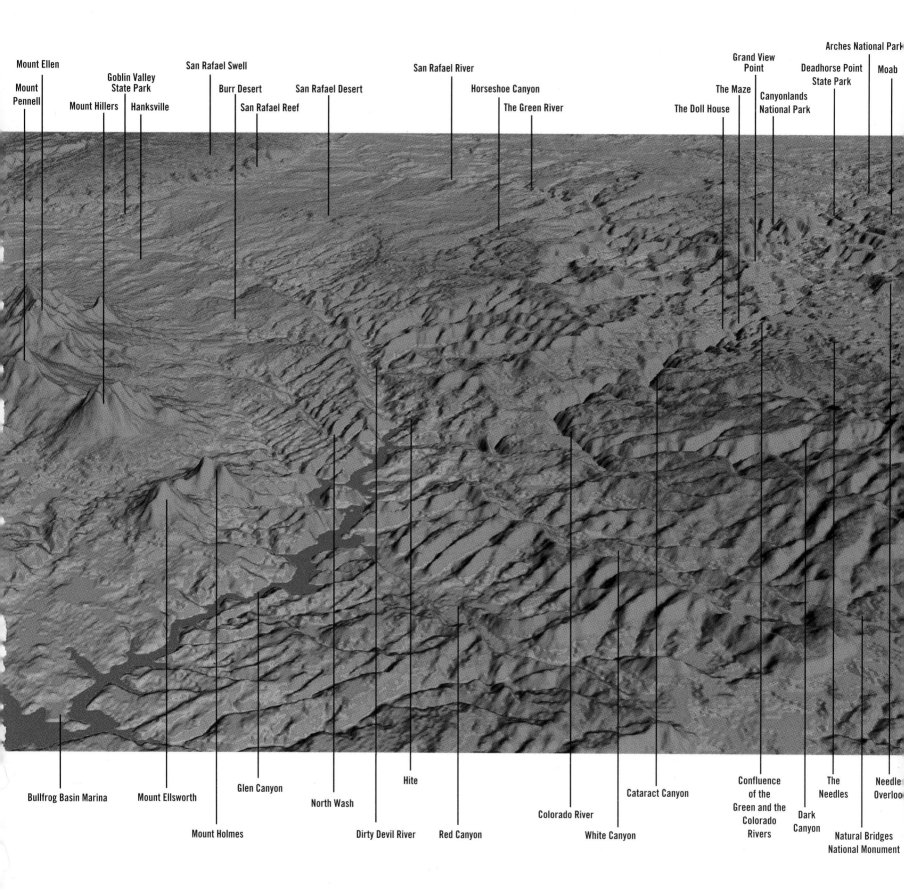

Mount Ellen

Mount Pennell

Mount Hillers

Goblin Valley State Park

Hanksville

San Rafael Swell

Burr Desert

San Rafael Reef

San Rafael Desert

San Rafael River

Horseshoe Canyon

The Green River

The Doll House

The Maze

Grand View Point

Canyonlands National Park

Deadhorse Point State Park

Arches National Park

Moab

Bullfrog Basin Marina

Mount Ellsworth

Mount Holmes

Glen Canyon

North Wash

Dirty Devil River

Hite

Red Canyon

Colorado River

White Canyon

Cataract Canyon

Confluence of the Green and the Colorado Rivers

Dark Canyon

Natural Bridges National Monument

The Needles

Needle Overlook

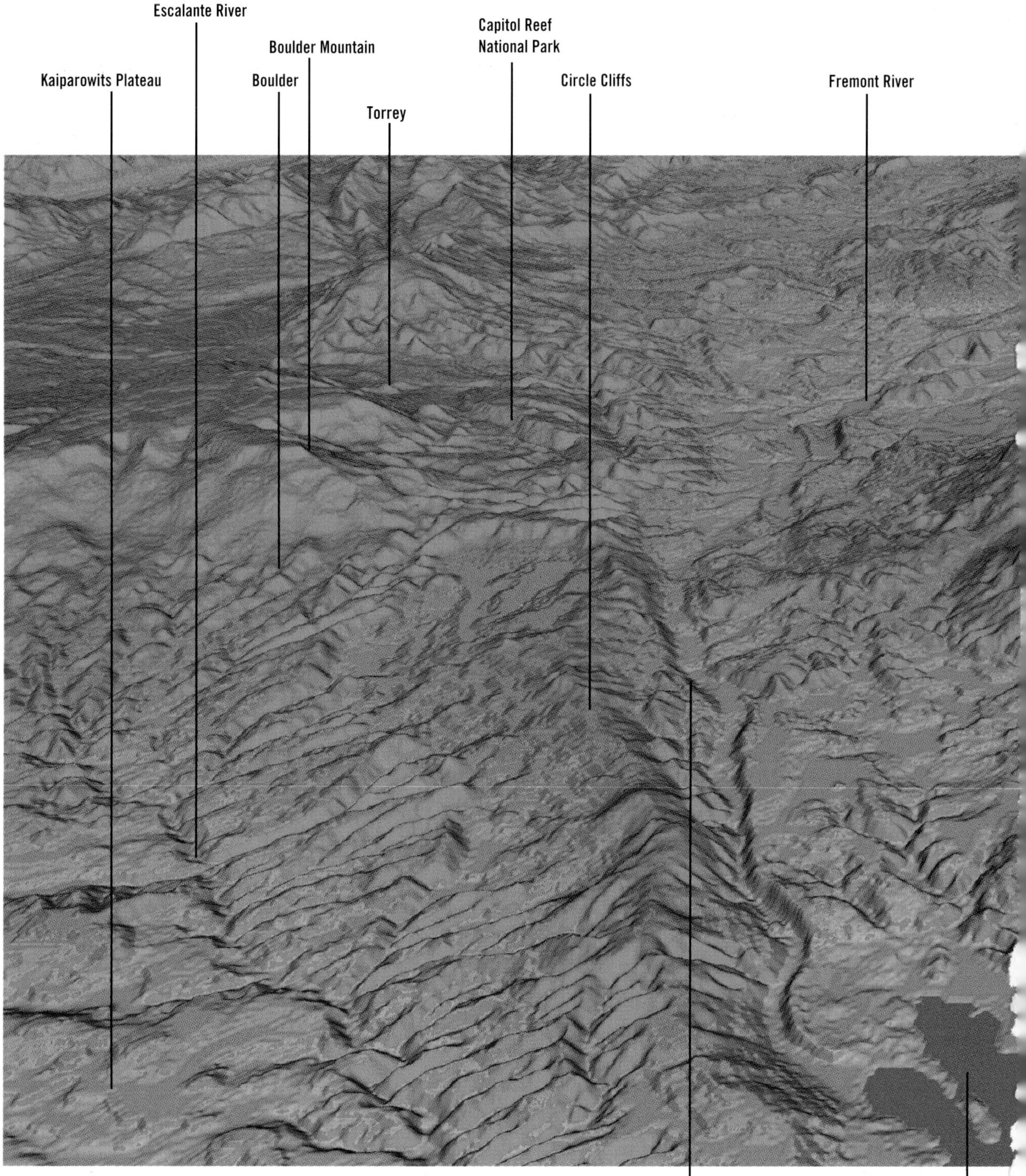

Escalante River

Capitol Reef
National Park

Boulder Mountain

Kaiparowits Plateau   Boulder   Circle Cliffs   Fremont River

Torrey

preserves some fifteen hundred head-turning, uncanny
punctures in the slickrock
member of the Entrada sandstone.

Of all the protected
areas in canyon country, Glen
Canyon National Recreation
Area encompasses the
largest piece, stretching from
Glen Canyon Dam (the barrier
creating Lake Powell) into
Cataract Canyon, grabbing
up the drainages of the
Escalante and San Juan
along the way.

Canyonlands National
Park sits in the bulls eye of
canyon country and is a maze
of just that—canyons. If one
park could represent the
region, it would probably be
Canyonlands, because of its

Waterpocket
Fold

Lake
Powell

diversity and great beauty. A small area south of   these great sandstone monuments may be the best-known fea-
Canyonlands—Natural Bridges National Monument—is an out-   ture in all of the canyon country landscape. Other protected areas
door showcase of water-eroded bridges of stone.   include Goblin Valley and the Goosenecks of the San

In Monument Valley, dramatic sandstone monoliths salute   Juan State Parks, as well as the Grand Gulch and Dark
thousands of visitors from all over the world every year; in fact,   Canyon Primitive Areas.

TOPOGRAPHY OF
SLICKROCK COUNTRY

The slickrock country of southeast Utah, often called the "Canyonlands" region, after the national park by the same name, is one of the most vividly colored expanses of eroded, bare rock in the world. The Colorado River slices right through it and cuts down into its Paleozoic heart. Together with the Green, San Juan, and Escalante rivers—its major tributaries—the Colorado carves a latticework of drainages that forms the erosional template for the whole region.

A good portion of canyon country is protected—either as a national park, national monument, state park, primitive area, tribal park, or other types of preserves. Capitol Reef National Park protects a linear strip of canyon country, a long wrinkle in the earth's surface called the Waterpocket Fold. Its upper section is the well-known Capitol Reef. On the other side of canyon country, Arches National Park

Navajo Arch in Arches National Park frames juniper and pinyon trees that have taken root in a pocket of sand between solid blocks of sandstone.

La Sal Mountains
La Sal
Newspaper Rock State Historical Monument
Dolores River
Edge of the Cedars State Park
Mount Linneaus
Blanding
Monticello
Hatch Wash
Castle Valley
Grand Gulch
Cedar Mesa
Abajo Mountains

Note: Although it may look like a photograph, this image is actually a computerized, extruded, topographic view. It was created using digital elevation models derived from the United States Geological Survey (USGS) satellite maps and traditional, flat USGS topography maps.

To prepare the extruded topo map, data from the USGS was downloaded from the Earth Science Information Center to a personal computer and converted into a three-dimensional model. There, a flat or "birds-eye" version was rendered which simulates a direct overhead view of the region (the end sheets on both inside covers of this book were reproduced from this version). The flat version was then tilted in order to create a view of the area from an angle 29 degrees off the horizon. Shadows, textures, and colors were added to represent a view that one might see from space.

DESERT VARNISH: THE SHEEN OF LIFE

D esert varnish gives a satinlike finish to a sheer Navajo sandstone cliff in the San Rafael Desert.

A s if the brilliant reds, oranges, and maroons of the sandstones in slickrock country were not enough, canyon walls are also adorned with the colors of desert varnish, an effect created by the work of bacteria and microfungi on rock surfaces.

Varnishes consist of airborne dust as well as clay particles left by water dripping down the canyon walls. Recently, geologists have shown that fungi and bacteria cement the clay and dust to the cliff faces, coloring the rock. Desert varnishes rich in iron may come in shades of dark red and deep rust. Those that are richer in manganese are satin-black and iridescent blue-black.

Look up, and there's a spindly tree somehow growing straight out of the cliff face. We've all seen one before, either in person or in some cartoon where a rattled cowboy or a hapless coyote is hanging on to it for dear life. And yet, every time we see its tenacious roots gaining purchase in the tiniest of cracks and crevices in sheer rock walls, we are hushed with awe. With all that rock, and so little soil, how did some stray seed ever work up the nerve to become a tree?

Just as rock climbers find toe holds in hairline fractures, certain plants have adapted to make use of the slightest cracks in slickrock. From pinyon pines and scrappy rock mat to maidenhair ferns and mosses, these hangers-on have evolved strategies for surviving the baldest of bedrocks.

Patterns of plant cover shift from place to place, from soil to soil. These patterns make up the pieces of an ecological puzzle that, when put together, provides a complete picture of the canyon country. Once you have the puzzle in mind, you can then go out and explore this landscape mosaic for the stories of how life came to cloak the largest exposure of bare rock on the continent.

* * *

Short, shrubby plants are well-suited to the arid conditions of the region, extending their root systems out laterally rather than growing tall stems. More than half the plants in canyon country are waist-height or lower.

One morning we passed through Monument Valley and continued north, feeling dazzled by the giant red rock hands and totem poles of that windswept landscape. We left the main road after a short distance, and after bouncing along a dusty dirt road for an hour or

INTO EVERY CREVICE
LIFE TAKING ROOT

so, looked to the west. A smooth, ivory ridge of Navajo sandstone dipped toward us as we paused to revel in the flush of wildflowers at our feet. Here in the deep sand of an ancient wash, there was still plenty of moisture to keep a half dozen types of wildflowers blooming and bobbing with bees: orange-pink globemallows, sulfur yellow prince's plume, powder-blue flax, and purple scurfpeas were among them. Up on the slickrock slope, only a lone rainbow cactus had blossoms this late in the spring. We headed up a steep wash thick with wolfberry, hackberry, and squawbush, then disappeared into the white sandstone.

After half an hour of hiking, a few miles past where we had left our car on the sandy flats, we entered the mouth of a cave the size of a basketball court. That mouth still murmured stories from thousands of years past.

Under a ledge along the edge of the cave mouth, we spotted an ancient text that recorded the local flora of past times. That text was not a book, but a midden—a mound of debris left by generations of packrats, the archivists of the Southwest. Over the last fourteen thousand years, untold numbers of packrats have foraged a hundred yards or so out from this cave, returning with samples of the surrounding plant life. They cached their booty in crevices inside the cave, which sheltered their dens and scat stations. When, by chance, their urine soaked into these seeds and stems, a crystallized crust formed that perfectly preserved the identity of most of the plants and associated insects. Each layer of matted-down plants and bugs can be accurately dated. However odd it may sound, packrat middens can crystallize a view of what vegetation was once like, much the way canyons enable us to view past geological episodes.

If we had visited our cave ten thousand years ago, we would have been surrounded by limber pine, Douglas fir, and Rocky Mountain juniper. Today, however, scrappy Utah junipers have replaced their cooler cousins from the Rocky Mountains. There is only one specimen of a pine tree—and at that, the driest version, the pinyon pine—dangling from a cliff above the cave.

Other plants such as prickly pear, Brigham tea, yucca, and squawbush have endured all the climatic changes of the last ten millennia and still grow beyond the cave mouth much as they did during the Ice Age. Perhaps because their growth forms make them so adaptable to climatic change, they have the luxury of sticking to one place when others must move on or die.

Plants and animals have had to "move on or die" numerous times in the past, whenever there was a dramatic change in climatic conditions. Some species persisted while others dropped out. Thanks to debris left by our furry friends, we can now get a sense of the plants that were lost and how others established themselves on rock and sand during the eras following the Ice Age.

Packrat middens have also helped dispel an early notion of why plants grow where they do that has been misleadingly codified in many trail guides, roadside signs, and museum displays throughout the West. That notion—the "life zone" concept—was formulated in the 1890s by Dr. C. Hart Merriam of the U.S. Department of Agriculture while he traveled through the Southwest. Merriam believed that elevation largely determines what grows where.

PACKRAT MIDDENS:
ARCHIVES OF THE SOUTHWEST

Not until thirty years ago did scientists realize that packrat middens—tangles of sticks and other plant material—are key to understanding how landscapes have changed over the centuries. Ecologist Phil Wells and entomologist Clive Jorgensen were the first to realize that the middens could answer some important questions.

The two scientists made the discovery one day when they were out conducting field research in the Nevada Mountains. They had been disappointed not to find a woodland of pinyon and juniper where they had expected to see one. Scrambling down into a limestone canyon, however, Jorgensen spotted a dark, shiny chunk of plant matter tucked beneath an overhang. It was

a packrat midden filled with a dense, luxuriant mass of juniper twigs. "This is where all the juniper is!" Jorgensen yelled to Wells.

When a laboratory radiocarbon dated their samples, Jorgensen and Wells discovered some of the juniper twigs came from trees that were alive as long as forty thousand years ago.

Based on the packrat evidence, the scientists theorized that eight thousand years ago, the climate was still cool enough that junipers could grow at least eighteen hundred feet lower than they do today. Then, as the effects of the Ice Age passed, warmer and drier times killed the low-lying junipers. The rest retreated to

higher climes, and the rocky slopes became scantily clad. Where the ancient junipers used to thrive, only hardy desert shrubs like saltbush and blackbrush survive today.

The packrat revolution that Wells and Jorgensen started in the 1960s was extended by Julio Betancourt in the 1970s. Working in the slickrock wildlands, Betancourt collaborated with packrats to record how the flora there had been reshuffled through the ages.

He firmly established that the mix of plants at various elevations was once very different than it is today. And he was able to link the changes in plant cover to climatic conditions that occured as long as fifteen thousand years ago, when half-mile-thick glaciers covered the mountain ranges just east of the Colorado Plateau.

The roots of desert shubs reach down into pockets of soil moisture among the fractured rocks of White Rim sandstone in Canyonlands National Park.

He focused on the fact that as you go up in elevation, rainfall increases and temperature decreases, and plants sort themselves out based on what they need in terms of moisture and temperature. He gained his fame on the southern edge of the Colorado Plateau by documenting a storybook sequence of life zones, riding horseback from the depths of the Grand Canyon up to the twelve-thousand-foot San Francisco Peaks.

Merriam's notion is, of course, partly true. Elevation is a very important determinant of habitat. However, limber pines once dominated entire forests as low as fifty-two hundred feet in elevation, while the few scattered limber pines you find today are above eighty-four hundred feet, in forests of white fir, Douglas fir, and prostrate juniper. Currently on the Colorado Plateau, limber pine forms no zone of its own as it did thousands of years ago. Ponderosa and pinyon pines can be found at lower elevations, but not with the same exact mix of understory shrubs that formerly grew in the shadows of limber pines. As the climate changed, new assortments of plants dominated different elevations; the same bunch seldom clustered together for long.

There is another reason that cohesive vegetation zones haven't moved up and down canyon walls, as Merriam proposed, in simple lock-step, with changes in temperature and rainfall: the distributions of plants in canyon country are strongly shaped by the underlying influence of rock. Where igneous rock dominates the Henry, La Sal, and Abajo Mountains, low desert shrub cover usually gives way to pygmy woodlands of juniper and pinyon when you reach fifty-two hundred to six thousand feet. But on Mancos shales—with poorer water-holding capacity and weirder chemistry—scrubby desert plants extend up to seventy-six hundred feet. The draughty conditions of Mancos shales keep junipers and other moisture-loving trees sixteen hundred feet higher up the slopes than they would be if they were growing in a different soil. Sixteen hundred feet is a mountain's worth of difference.

There *are* identifiable communities of plants and animals in canyon country, but they are shaped as much by rock and soil as they are by elevation. And, as the packrat middens tell us, the cohesiveness of each community through time is tenuous. Most associations of plants in canyon country are more like jam sessions than they are like long-established orchestras.

* * *

One of our favorite places to pause for a sundown dinner is on the sandy mesas on the Island in the Sky in Canyonlands. While our campstove heated water for Spanish rice and beans one late afternoon on the Island, we walked the benches of Navajo sandstone and tallied up the kinds of plants growing in the sandy pockets between. The sand could look no redder, the foliage no greener than they did that evening. But despite the brilliance of the reds, the greens were more abundant than we had expected. This was no desert of barren, shifting sands. It was a wonderland of feathery grasses bent over by the bounty of their seedheads, of shrubs three times their normal size, of white evening primroses and ivory sand verbenas that bloom for weeks after the last rains have passed. These deep pockets of sand underlain by stone held moisture sufficient to support a lush grassland.

Dig down below the top eight inches of dry, sugary sand, and you will find that each successive layer acts as a miniature aquifer. These layers of sand hold moisture that is much more

PROTECTING THE LIVING CRUSTS
OF CANYON COUNTRY

*P*erhaps only on the Colorado Plateau can you find a right-to-life movement for lichens, mosses, green algae, cyanobacteria, and microfungi. Ecologists there have found that tiny communities in this arid land form microscopic "living crusts" called cryptogamic soil or microbiotic crusts. These delicate communities comprise three quarters of the soil cover of canyon country and, in many ways, "hold the whole place in place."

A prominent member of these ground-cover communities is cyanobacteria, also known as filament-forming blue-green algae. This microbe—made up of thin filaments surrounded by sticky sheaths that cling to soil particles—plays an essential role in stabilizing desert soil and preventing erosion. Thanks to the work of Colorado Plateau ecologist Jane Belnap, efforts are being made in canyon country to preserve these fragile living crusts, whose structures can be severely damaged for many years when they are crushed beneath the weight of hooves, boots, or automobile tires.

readily available to plant roots than the water held in silt or clay. While clay can hold more moisture, the electrical charges of its molecules tenaciously retain the water, resisting its release to thirsty roots.

Because of the paradoxical capacity of dunes to retain moisture even during droughts, their vegetative cover is much more lush than that found on nearby gravel, hardpan, or clay. Dune-adapted perennials can rapidly extend their roots and shoots through sand and often form a mound of multiple stems rather than one treelike trunk. Along Mill Creek outside of Moab, we once measured a single squawbush, emerging from a dune, that had hundreds of little shoots that covered an eight-by-twenty-foot oval. If the dune began to move, new squawbush shoots would follow its course. In this way, the shrub would never be left high and dry by a shifting dune as a tree with a single trunk might be. The plants which have made some accommodation in their lifestyles to the shifting sands beneath them often suffer far less stress than those that cast their lot on more permanent substrates.

* * *

In contrast to the dunes, the toughest rocks and soils for plants in the West are those of the Mancos, Chinle, and Tropic shales. The shaley soils have stopped many an extravagant life—one used to living on unlimited water—dead in its tracks. Shrubs and wildflowers that are otherwise ubiquitous in the region simply can't gain a foothold on the intractable shales.

We explored the Mancos one day, after driving north out of Arches National Park toward a ghost of a town named Thompson. We walked among these scruffy devil plants. "The soil just baaaakes up here on this slope," one of our companions moaned. The light's intensity made everything look overexposed, from his pallid complexion to the pale gray plants around him.

Of the shales, Mancos is the most notorious for making a plant's life miserable. Perhaps because Mancos was set down under conditions exactly opposite those of the sandstones, it's not surprising that it produces an altogether different flora. Unlike the breezy dunes and free-flowing streams that shaped the colorful sandstones, stagnant and oxygen-poor waters gave us the sulfurous, gray-black muds and limes of the Mancos. When finally reexposed to oxygen and to rain, Mancos runs through a chain of chemical reactions that produces everything from sulfuric acid and gypsum nodules to saline- and sodium-rich crusts. Mancos chemistry can get more sour than unsweetened lemonade and saltier than the rim around a margarita glass.

The toxic brew of chemicals that characterizes Mancos and Tropic shales is rough enough on most plants, but the physical properties of its clays are shocking to even the hardiest of them. When it rains, a topsoil loaded with these clays rapidly expands with moisture until it seals itself off with a slick cap that lets no more water pass. This cap loses moisture rapidly, shrinking so severely that deep fissures are left in the soil. Even when a seed germinates on the slick gumbo cap of these shales, its roots can seldom get past this seal, so the seed dries up when the clays begin to contract. The deep cracks that form in Mancos or Tropic clays during droughts ruin oxygen exchange with plant roots, wreaking havoc on the few plants hardy enough to penetrate the caps and get established. No wonder one of these hardy vegetables has been dubbed "Last Chance Townsendia."

FOLLOWING PAGES:

Patches of aspen dominate the higher reaches of pine forests in the Abajo, La Sal, and Henry Mountains.

Mancos and Tropic shales make for a poor stand of plants at any altitude, but at lower elevations, they can and do attract enough low-growing, salt-loving, hell-raising shrubs, forbs, and cacti to form some semblance of desertscrub vegetation. In fact, Mancos and Tropic shales host a greater proportion of the region's one hundred and twenty endemic plants than do other soils.

* * *

Like shales, limestones and gypsums also lend a certain austerity to canyon country vegetation, and their slopes host quite a few of the same species that survive on the shales. Desert trumpet, tiquilia, shadscale, snakeweed, and globemallow are among them. But gypsum has its own peculiar set of colonizers as well, some of which can tolerate or even thrive where selenium—a toxic mineral associated with uranium—concentrates in the gypsum plugs of the Paradox formation. Locoweeds, sego lilies, nodding onions, and peppergrass join the ubiquitous prince's plume on gypsum slopes, for all of them tolerate or favor gypsum rich in selenium. On both the crunchy slopes of Prommel Dome and the gypsum knolls just above the Moab Slough, we felt as though we had arrived at a paradox where plants thrived by downing poisons.

In contrast to the gypsum poison-takers, salt-loving extremists dominate the vegetation around certain oasislike springs and seeps in canyon country. There, sodium-rich "black alkali" soils take their color from the dark, organic-rich humus particles that are separated out and moved upward to the surface by sodium molecules. These oases are usually barren in the center, where salts are most concentrated, but they are surrounded by luxuriant rings of greasewood, pickleweed, seepweed, and saltgrass. If running water comes along frequently enough, willow, salt cedar, cattail, and sedge may move in to make the rings lusher.

In an oasis such as this, just before the slickrock climbs up to Delicate Arch in Arches National Park, we saw a gathering of these salt-imbibing maniacs. They do not form a large patch of vegetation, but they are so peculiarly verdant when compared to the surrounding plant cover that they might as well be aliens from another planet.

There are two other kinds of oases in canyon country. The first is found in slickrock drainages, where bedrock depressions fill with water from winter snowmelts or summer rains. The bedrock depressions, called "potholes," were historically known as *tinajas*, a word coming to us from Spanish explorers who relied on such waterholes for survival. When these potholes are shallow enough that you must literally suck their water while sprawled on your belly, they are termed "kiss tanks." Other bedrock depressions are larger and go by a variety of additional names.

Tinajas host an assortment of plants that regularly sprout on any well-watered spot. Cattails, carrizo reedgrass, Gooding's willows, and birchleaf buckthorns rim the natural tanks. Understory herbs add a profusion of flowers—and the bees and butterflies they attract. Paintbrush, goldenrod, purple asters, and thistles bloom wildly among the florid green backdrops of panicgrass, horsetails, and rushes. Occasionally, a tinaja will be large and deep enough to keep a cottonwood at its side, although the tree may be a mere bonsai compared to those growing downstream by the nearest river bend.

*S*lopes of Tropic shale, viewed here near the Kaiparowits Plateau, are only sparsely covered with plant life because the shaley soil contains a witches' brew of chemicals toxic to most plants.

Pygmy woodlands consist of mostly short-statured pinyon pines and junipers at midelevations.

Below timberline, patches of aspen mingle with subalpine forests of fir and spruce.

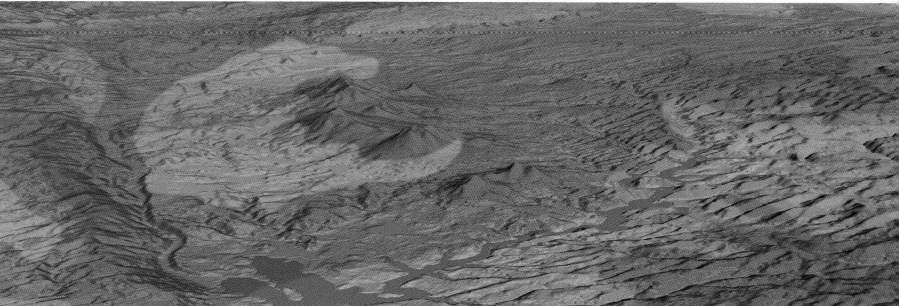

Mat saltbush is one of the few plants which not only survives but thrives on Mancos shale.

Blackbrush dominates dry but relatively stable slopes down to the lowest elevations in canyon country.

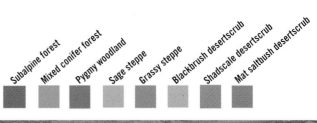

VEGETATION OVERLAY

Subalpine forest   Mixed conifer forest   Pygmy woodland   Sage steppe   Grassy steppe   Blackbrush desertscrub   Shadscale desertscrub   Mat saltbush desertscrub

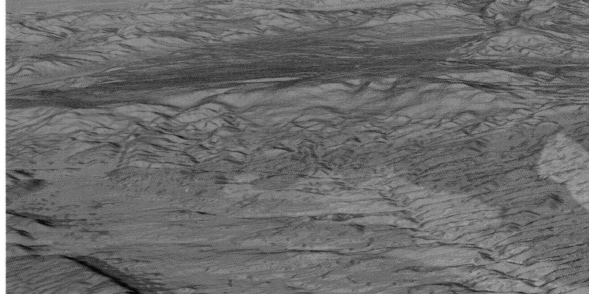

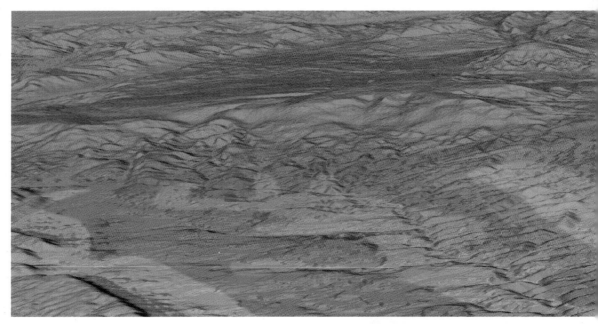

thrown into the pot: flooding or freezing, rainshadows or saline seeps, grazing or grasshoppers.

Compare these two slanted, birds-eye views of the slickrock wildlands, simulated by computers from topographic maps—one color-coded for geology, the other to indicate vegetation. You can see how the distributions of the vegetation types follow—or in some places, diverge from—the underlying rock types. In both images, Lake Powell ranges from bottom-center to dead-center and is surrounded by desertscrub on Jurassic period sandstones. To the far right, the volcanic rocks of the Abajos and the La Sals are cloaked in coniferous forests. On the far left, the Aquarius Plateau rises from pygmy woodlands into extensive coniferous forests beyond the western margins of canyon country.

Grassy steppe, with its characteristic yuccas and Brigham tea, covers vast portions of Utah's mesas and plains.

LANDSCAPE ECOLOGY—
LINKING PLANT COVER TO SOILS

The sparse cover of green, gray, and brown vegetation that colors canyon country is just as remarkable as all its naked rock. There are large mappable expanses of eight vegetation types, from the depths of the canyons to the alpine tundras of the tallest mountains. With some ten thousand feet of vertical range, you can explore rock and root from desertscrub to subalpine forest.

Looking out over the region, it seems that plant cover in some spots changes in simple lock-step with soil type or elevation range. Mat saltbush loves the Mancos shale. Shadscale's grays cover much of the Morrison formation. Sandy soils weathered from great sandstones like the Navajo or Entrada sandstone host bunch grasses of the semiarid steppe. Mixes of conifers, aspens, and oaks form mosaics on the talus slopes of laccolithic peaks, like those in the Henry Mountains. Where soil and flora shift at the same pace, along the same abrupt elevational transitions, nature's patterns seem simple and elegantly orderly. Yet such sharp delineations are not always the case. In some plant communities, a change in soil may only change plant densities or the mix of wildflowers underfoot, but not the dominant plant cover. Elsewhere, plants may change not because of different soil types, but because other factors get

Low shrubs dominate much of the vegetation cover in canyon country.

Big sage mixes with Indian rice to form grassy steppe, but also covers parklands in pygmy woodlands.

Ponderosa pines mix with other conifers as well as oaks and aspen to form tall forests on mountain slopes.

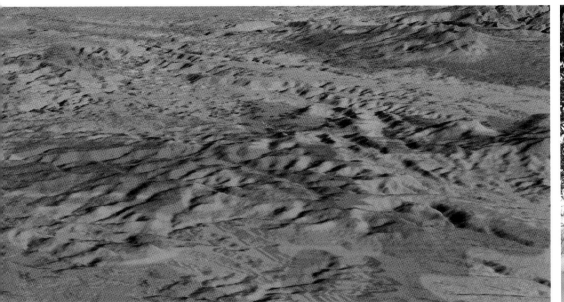

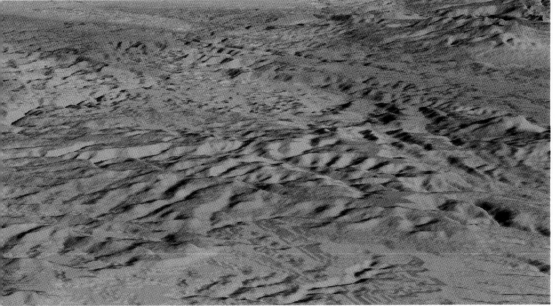

Below these ranges and plateaus are large expanses of sedimentary rock types: the red beds of the Permian period; the shales and siltstones of the Triassic period, including extensive patches of Moenkopi and Chinle formations; Jurassic period rocks that originated in dunes or streams; and the sediments of the Cretaceous period, dominated by Mancos shale.

A change in plant cover can predict a change in rock type—or even hint at the presence of uranium. Conversely, a change in soil color and texture can be an indicator of a "new" set of plants.

In this way, canyon country hues can signal ecological transitions and soil and plant shifts: the muddy reds and browns of the Moenkopi are linked with the red-brown cedar bark on juniper trunks, and the grayish golds of Mancos shale are tied to the yellow-green of prince's plume.

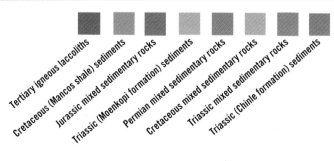

ROCK GEOGRAPHY

Tertiary igneous laccoliths
Cretaceous (Mancos shale) sediments
Jurassic mixed sedimentary rocks
Triassic (Moenkopi formation) sediments
Permian mixed sedimentary rocks
Cretaceous mixed sedimentary rocks
Triassic mixed sedimentary rocks
Triassic (Chinle formation) sediments

The third kind of oasis in canyon country is the hanging garden, what the foremost Utah botanist Stanley Welsh hails as "a well-watered island in an ocean of drought." Try walking for days down the gravely bed of a drought-stricken canyon, then come around a corner to a dripping spring cloaked in verdure. Chances are, it will sweep your breath away. A plunge pool beneath a hanging garden is to a backpacker what a flame is to a moth.

Hanging gardens spring to life in alcove-forming sandstones such as Navajo and Entrada. But don't let that stop you from looking for them elsewhere, for they have also been found in Bluff sandstone, the Kayenta formation, the White Rim sandstone in Canyonlands, and the Cedar Mesa sandstone at Natural Bridges.

Hanging gardens occur where a trickle of water squeaks out of a joint in the rock like a leak around a pipe fixture. Such joints offer outlets for drips, seeps, or gushing cascades. Whether shaped as an alcove, a window-blind, or a hanging ledge, hanging gardens attract a variety of water-loving plants. Many of them are more characteristic of mountain lakes or marshlands in the tall grass prairie than they are of desert country.

In fact, hanging gardens harbor a remarkably large percentage of canyon country flora, given the small amount of space they occupy. For example, more than a tenth of all the kinds of algae in Utah have been found in just forty postage-stamp-size clusters of hanging gardens in southern Utah. The hanging garden is a sanctuary for a suprising number of rare species, a few of them threatened. Although their habitat is minuscule in size, the kachina daisy, the alcove death camas, the bog orchid, the giant Rydberg's thistle, and the Navajo sedge are among the special plants that cling to the dripping walls of canyons as their only hope for survival.

Late one summer evening, a good while after the sun had gone down behind the Fiery Furnace, we felt our way along a wall of Entrada sandstone. Although it was almost too dark to see one another as anything more than shadows, we could see in front of us something glistening with the little bit of light still reflecting off the rocks. We stood frozen for a moment and listened to the sounds of dripping water playing a subtle symphony in a miniature amphitheater. We moved into the tiny alcove and became audience to the Rhapsody of the Weeping Rock.

As we reached up and touched the drip line, we could feel the coolness and smell the muskiness of its players: maidenhair fern, monkeyflower, alcove daisy, golden sedge, and scratchgrass. There was salt on their brows, but they kept on playing, swaying in the evening breeze. A few salty droplets cascaded through the foliage before plinking themselves down on the algae-slimed rock. We thought we heard a Woodhouse's toad bring in the bass line from somewhere hidden in the maidenhairs. As we turned away from the rock, a low-swooping poorwill flew before us; its call notes punctuated the symphony's finale.

POTHOLES AND KIPUKAS:
LIVING WITH A DEPRESSION

Depressions in the rock that hold rainwater (following pages) are called potholes, and they come in a variety of sizes. Tinajas are often about bathtub size, waterpockets are somewhat larger, and weathering pits are giant-size catchments up to a hundred yards wide.

With any of these rock depressions, just add water and you have an instant aquatic ecosystem, chock full of algae, amphibians, crustaceans, snails, and insect larvae. Gnats, mosquito larvae, and tadpoles can survive in temporary pools persisting as little as two weeks. Fairy shrimp, however, require a longer season of fresh water. Toads and aquatic insects such as backswimmers need permanent pools to survive or must migrate to other potholes if theirs dries up.

If sand and other sediments accumulate in the bedrock-lined depressions, the pools may be replaced by dry islands of a few herbs, grasses, and shrubs that can root in shallow soils. As the soil deepens, more dryland plants will colonize the bedrock pockets. Native Hawaiians have their own word for these islands of plant growth in barren rock: kipukas.

LOOKING FOR LOST WORLDS ATOP MESAS AND BUTTES

A hanging garden is a kind of oasis found in slickrock country where seeps emerge from cracks in canyon walls or springs flow out in modest trickles from cliff bases. Mosses and flowering plants cling to vertical walls and find footholds below overhangs. Maidenhair fern, pictured here, is one of the most common residents of hanging gardens.

For years, ecologists wondered if the isolated, steep-walled mesas and buttes of canyon country might harbor unique forms and communities of life. By 1960, several scientists had reached the tops of many of these promontories to find out the answer—but to their initial disappointment, they discovered no "lost worlds" of extinct animals and plant species. What they did find, however, was healthy, undisturbed vegetation—protected from the effects of grazing by the sheer walls, too steep for cows to climb. They also found a resident mammal—the canyon mouse. When ecologists helicoptered to the top of the Jug, a remote butte on the White Rim, canyon mice were the only native mammals they encountered. The tiny mice had scaled almost five hundred feet of sheer Wingate cliffs to find a habitat free of competing rodents. To that colony of canyon mice, the Jug was not a lost world. It was home.

O ur pickup truck lurched for a moment on a steep incline, then climbed in low gear until it reached an elevation of nine thousand feet in the La Sal Mountains. We killed the engine, set the emergency brake, and got out of the truck. We faced west and gazed out over the glorious chaos of it all: the outrageous mess of landforms and lifeforms comprising the slickrock wildlands.

We were up in a mountain meadow of rainbow colors: powder blue iris, violet lupines, and pink roses edging a forest of quaking aspen, ponderosa, and Douglas fir. Behind us, toward the highest peaks of the La Sals, we could see nothing but tundra and subalpine forests in the shadow of steel-gray clouds laced with lightning. If we did an about-face, below us, to the west, there were enough sunbeams streaming between the clouds to highlight a whole range of other habitats.

Immediately below the mountain meadow, we could see what looked like a chenille bedspread: little, regularly spaced clumps of green— the pygmy woodlands of eight- to twenty-foot-tall pinyon and juniper trees. In parklike meadows tucked into those pygmy woodlands, big sage and Brigham tea formed dense gray islands.

At an elevation below the pygmy woodlands, thorny mosaics of desertscrub and grassy steppe spread across a buff-colored expanse. Even farther below, in the Moab Valley below gorgeous red cliffs, we could see a few ribbons of

D esertscrub vegetation spills down the slopes of a drainage in the Escalante Basin. Pocket-sized riparian groves of trees flourish in drainages where sufficient water is available.

CARVING A NICHE
WILDLIFE HABITATS OF CANYON AND MOUNTAIN

green. We wondered whether these were riparian forests of cottonwood and willow which bless the edges of streams, or salt cedars which curse them.

There were a few lives we couldn't easily see from this lofty vantage point. Among them were the insects, birds, mammals, and reptiles that weave this wildly colored tapestry together. Each of the habitats we could spot from our promontory in the La Sal Mountains has its own characteristic wildlife-in-residence, some of them conspicuous, others cryptic. We would need a lot of time and plenty of luck to encounter the entire menagerie of the slickrock wildlands.

* * *

Whether we saw them or not, a third of all wildlife species on the Colorado Plateau is found only in mountainous uplands like the La Sals. Another third is confined to riparian corridors along streams and rivers. The last third is comprised of ubiquitous critters like mule deer and deer mice, mountain bluebirds and Cassin's finches, all of whom spend time in high country like the La Sals but are commonly found elsewhere as well, depending on the severity of the season. They can sometimes be found around mountain parklands, but are also spotted in riparian forests of the lowlands. These animals serve as the connective tissue between one habitat and another, dispersing seeds, pollinating flowers, or opening patches in forests so that meadow plants can grow. They are seldom so allegiant to just one habitat that they refuse to set foot into another.

Trouble is, you can map rocks—you can even map vegetation types—but few animals will stand still long enough to earn nailed-down spots on a map. That's why the dynamics of plant-animal interactions in the canyons of color make for stories wilder than what any habitat map can tell us. That's also why we resist giving out simple recipes for habitat types in canyon country until it becomes clear how dynamic—how imbued by animal spirits— the natural boundaries between different habitats can be.

Animals don't simply walk out onto a stage that has already been decorated with plants and begin their existence there. The truth is, they actually help design their eco- logical theater by disturbing the soil, altering the flow of water, selectively culling some plants out of the vegetation, or in other ways changing the dynamics of their neighborhood. Canyon country habitats echo with dialogues between beaver and cottonwood, prairie dog and galleta grass, Clark's nutcracker and pinyon pine.

Biogeographers can only map vegetation, but the habitat tapestry is always more complex. If you think in terms of biotic communities, the often hidden animals are just as impor- tant as the plants. Jim Brown, a Southwestern biogeographer, found this out first-hand when he removed all the kangaroo rats from a section of desert scrubland to see what would happen.

Twelve years after the kangaroo rats (K-rats, for short) were taken out, the density of grasses had increased threefold, and large-seeded spring wildflowers had increased a

A coyote pauses, alert to the movement of a small mammal in the grass. Coyotes range through most habitats in the slickrock wildlands and are found in the stories of the Navajo, Paiute, and Hopi.

A lone mule deer wanders out of the forest to a shallow pool at dusk. Mule deer herds may have as many as seventy animals foraging together in the meadows and coniferous forests of the mountain ranges of canyon country.

thousandfold. With all those seeds handy, you might guess that seed-eating birds also became more abundant. But the fact is, they decreased in density because they couldn't find many seeds, since the formerly barren ground was now thick with grass and plant litter. And because no one was around to keep up the neighborhood's K-rat mound-and-burrow topography, the scrubland lizards that love those elevated mounds also decreased.

Brown's study showed that the kangaroo rat was the "keystone species" of the whole biotic community—the prevailing force that kept it scrubby and desertlike. With the K-rats, he got a desertscrub. Without them, his desertscrub became a grassland.

* * *

There are other eco-dramas in canyon country similar to the kangaroo rat story. One involves the white-tailed prairie dog who lives on the "grassy steppe," a rich grassland of the Colorado Plateau found between four and five thousand feet in elevation. The prairie dogs' presence decreases some species (grasses and arthropods), but increases others (reptiles, birds, and mammals). Since prairie dog holes and weak-ankled cows do not mix well, it is not surprising that some Utah ranchers have tried to get rid of the prairie dogs—but removing them affects the whole community of the steppe.

Above the grasslands of the prairie dogs—at slightly higher elevations in canyon country (up to fifty-five hundred feet)—yuccas and grasses still grow, but they make room for big sage, black sagebrush, bushmint, and shinnery oak on the deeper soils of the steppe. Pygmy woodlands surround these grassy sagebrush parks. Pinyon pine is a dominant of the woodlands, and its edible pine nuts are relished by most mammals. As a result, when the pine nut supply increases during years of heavy rain, there are subsequent explosions in woodland rodent populations.

One of the key rodents of the sage park and woodland communities, the deer mouse, has been unfairly turned into the villain of the slickrock wildlands in recent years. This little rodent was identified as the primary carrier of the dreaded Four Corners hantavirus in 1993, when this respiratory disease suddenly killed more than two dozen people on the Colorado Plateau. The hantavirus outbreak coincided with the El Niño years of heavy rains in 1992 and 1993, which produced bumper crops of pine nuts.

Although it may seem contrary to what you would expect, medicine men among Native American tribes on the Colorado Plateau have traditionally viewed bumper crops as bad omens. Disease outbreaks akin to the hantavirus scare have occurred before in connection with bumper crops. These outbreaks have escaped the notice of the Western medical community, but not of Native American healers. Even though scientists had long ago made the connection between bumper crops and booms in rodent populations, it wasn't until the summer of 1993 that they connected the incidence of hantavirus cases to pinyon-nut gathering camps. They confirmed that deer mice and packrats were the carriers.

*C*lose cousins of stream-loving cotton-woods, aspens grow in clones at the higher elevations of canyon country.

A view of the west side of the

Waterpocket Fold (Capitol Reef

section), with the Henry

Mountains in the background.

Desert bighorn browse

on shrubs and cacti in the

cliffs and canyons.

Southwest.

From top to bottom, we typically see the following biotic communities of plants and animals: alpine tundra, subalpine coniferous forest with patches of aspen; mixed conifers in mosaics with oak, aspen, and sage; pygmy woodlands of pinyon pines and junipers; sage steppe; grassy steppe; and desertscrub. In this panoramic photo, the coniferous forests with their elk, black bear, and Clark's nutcrackers are found only in the highest mountain ranges. Pronghorns and prairie dogs colonize the grassy expanses on mesas and plains above the canyons. Rattlesnakes and hummingbirds may be found in a variety of habitats both above and below the canyon walls, while beavers make their homes in the perennial streams that pour down from the mountains and through the canyons.

Rattlesnakes are as much grassland and woodland dwellers as they are desert denizens.

BIOTIC COMMUNITIES
IN THE SLICKROCK WILDLANDS

Many complex communities of life are nestled into the slickrock landscape. In fact, the deep canyons and varied soils of slickrock wildlands bring many diverse communities within unusually close reach of one another. For example, in a matter of ten miles, it's possible to see subalpine forest communities, which are typical of Canada, next to communities that are characteristic of Mexico, such as desertscrub.

The pikas of the subalpine forest and desert cottontails of the desertscrub have entirely different temperature tolerances and strategies for survival, yet they can be reached within the same day's hike. Nowhere else on the continent is the accordion of life as tightly squeezed as it is within the uplands of the American

A *canyon pond in the Escalante Basin.*

The Clark's nutcracker caches
thousands of pine nuts each
year in the pygmy woodlands.

Prairie dog colonies
reshape vegetation in
the grassy steppe.

Hummingbirds migrating from Mexico pollinate woodland and meadow wildflowers.

Black bears move among streams, alpine meadows, and coniferous forests in mountain ranges.

Once widespread, antelope have been overhunted, but their population has recently recovered on the plateaus.

Formerly abundant, beaver now persist in a few reaches of perennial streams and wetlands.

Poison ivy, the bane of many canyon country hikers, sprawls over rocks along shady river-banks of the Escalante Basin, where water is present at least part of the year.

Fortunately for Colorado Plateau residents, the droughts in 1994 crippled the rodent populations, and the incidence of the disease has now plummeted. If anything, the story of the deer mouse and hantavirus gives insight into how vegetation responds to brief climatic changes—and how animal populations respond to vegetation shifts.

* * *

The chenille bedspreads of the pinyon and juniper pygmy woodlands can be found as low as five thousand feet, but typically grow from sixty-two hundred to seventy-eight hundred feet. This is the elevation range which occurs over the largest swath of canyon country. It is a playground especially suited for pinyon jays, ravens, and plain titmice.

While junipers take over the lower elevations of pygmy woodland, pinyon dominates at the higher reaches, after junipers drop out. Pinyon—the shortest and scrappiest of the six pines native to Utah—tends to climb upward until it overlaps with other pines, but it prefers more southerly exposures if it has to grow at higher elevations.

This habitat overlap among various kinds of pine is just where the pine-nut fanatic, Clark's nutcracker, loves to live. Clark's nutcracker will harvest nuts from pinyon and limber pine and, less frequently, from ponderosa pine and Douglas fir—but buries much of its booty instead of immediately consuming it. A single bird will "plant" over thirty thousand nuts from various conifers in one year. Being able to recall the location of as many as seven thousand separate caches has earned Clark's nutcracker its nickname, the Memory Bird. Even though its recall is astounding, it is sometimes unable to return to its caches. But the forest benefits from these leftovers—nutcracker plantings are important components of the regeneration of pines in southwest woodlands.

As you leave the pygmy woodland and move up the mountain slope on most ranges in the West, you'll move into large ponderosa pine forests. While there are indeed ponderosas on Navajo Mountain and in the Henry, La Sal, and Abajo ranges between seven thousand and ninety-eight hundred feet, they seldom develop into extensive, uniform stands as they do elsewhere. Instead, patches of ponderosa form mosaics with stands of other upland plants: quaking aspen, sage, Gambel oak, and a mixed stand of prostrate juniper, limber pine, and Douglas fir. These mosaics support surprisingly large herds of deer, which can be seen foraging for the first herbs of springtime on the ridges of the Abajos.

The highest reaches of the La Sals are loaded with little glacially carved lakes and meadows that also attract mule deer and elk. It must be too cold (or maybe too damp) for ponderosas up there because they become scarce after nine thousand feet; aspens fill in the gaps. One evening at twilight, as deer browsed in the aspen meadow near our camp at ninety-three hundred feet, we heard the banter of coyotes and then the bugling of elk not long after we started dinner. The aspens around our camp shimmered like silver columns in the reflected light after sundown. Trout sizzled on the campfires, and our nostrils picked up the acrid scent of

Brigham tea (left), a member of the joint-fir family, has been used medicinally by various cultures in canyon country for centuries.

Even the sparsest plant cover (left) on the shale slopes of the Chinle formation hosts a variety of rodents, lizards, and invertebrates.

aspen smoke and the rotting smells of the moist forest floor. The eyelike knobs on the aspen bark made it seem as though we were surrounded by thousands of watchful souls. Here, in the high country, it was easy to forget that the hot, dry, red rock desertscrub was only two hours and thirty-five miles away.

On the north-facing slopes above the lakes and aspen meadows, subalpine fir, white fir, and Engelmann spruce leave the pines and Douglas firs behind at around ninety-five hundred feet. This is the land of the red-breasted nuthatch, the dark-eyed junco, and the Townsend's solitaire. And beyond the calls of these birds is the least likely biotic community in all of the Colorado Plateau—the gang of tough, tundra-loving mat plants and high country critters that hang out just above tree line. There, above ten thousand feet, the subalpine forest drops away and the wind cruelly deforms the last of the trees aspiring to greater stature, treating all living things with a certain harshness. Of all the mountains in southeast Utah, only the La Sals have good tundra development above the spruces and firs. Mount Peale—at 12,721 feet—and its partner a few miles to the east, Tukuhnikivatz—at 12,483 feet—are high enough to leave most plants and animals behind. Pikas and marmots may delight at living in the land above the trees, but the rest of us mortals seldom think of their homes as a habitable dwelling place.

* * *

There is one other habitat that clashes even more with our mental image of slickrock wildlands—the humid, sluggish wetland of the slough. Only one fully developed slough exists anywhere in canyon country—in the Moab Valley where Mill Creek flows into a meander of the Colorado River and creates a patchwork of wet marsh, gallery forest of cottonwood, and salt cedar thickets. Also called tamarisk, salt cedar is a quick-growing, exotic shrub that has become ubiquitous in the Southwest. Less than a century after its introduction, it has succeeded in crowding out many native species.

If there was ever a habitat mosaic shaped by the presence of an animal, this is it—the slough—and the animal is the beaver. Eighty years ago beavers were few in number at the Moab Slough and there were virtually no salt cedars on the big, open sandy benches that edge the river. Since then, both beavers and salt cedars have been steadily increasing.

Recent wildlife management decisions at the Moab Slough have encouraged beavers to take up residence. But beavers are risky tenants. They have nearly decimated the cottonwood populations within the slough while gathering poles for their dams and mounds, and the aggressive salt cedars have moved in. As a result, many cottonwood-loving insect-eaters such as ash-throated flycatchers and kingbirds are finding fewer and fewer places to build their nests.

"The real dilemma is not that beavers are eating cottonwoods. They have always done that. It's that the cottonwoods haven't regenerated rapidly enough in recent

PLANT INFLUENCES ON ROCK

Monkey flower is found in moist, shady spots.

It's well known that soil type influences plants—but it's also true that plants affect the rock and soil in which they grow. Plant roots, for example, find hidden pockets of dampness within deep cracks in the rock and extend their root hairs and branchlets toward the moisture. When the roots enlarge, they eventually crack and wedge apart the layers of rock.

Plants also interact chemically with the soils in which they grow. For instance, needle and leaf litter from pines, oaks, and junipers can gradually neutralize certain salts in the soil, increasing its acidity.

A beaver pond in
the Escalante water-
shed.

years," explained Sue Bellagama, one of The Nature Conservancy's most dedicated workers in canyon country.

Cottonwood regeneration has suffered from decades of overgrazing. A few seedlings emerged following the floods in 1983 and 1984, but still missing are the intermediate generations of cottonwoods. A variety of ages must be present in order to sustain cottonwood forests over the long haul.

When the next flush of cottonwood regeneration will come along is one thing that neither the beavers nor the slough stewards can predict. And yet, the temporary lack of cottonwoods is not a failure of the preserve. What is being protected there is not merely a cottonwood forest but the dynamic potential for the beaver, cottonwood, and some one hundred fifty birds to be present in the slough at some time in the future, either sequentially or simultaneously. The floods will continue to come when we least expect them. The beaver populations will boom and bust. Cottonwood stands may dwindle for a while and then recolonize when we're not looking. But all of them have a standing invitation to stay at the slough whenever they can.

The uncertainty about whether they will come and stay next year or not until a decade from now is part of the glorious chaos of this country. If it were all that predictable, we'd never throw our sleeping bags on the ground, hike into its canyons just to see what's there, or test our rafts in its waters. Slickrock country serves up a powerful dose of chaos nearly every day—the dynamic nature of its habitat mosaics is testimony to that. Fortunately, there are lives which thrive on such chaos. The slickrock wildlands are filled with the best of the survivors and thrivers, from prince's plumes and aspen groves to prairie dogs and deer mice. And they bless us with their presence.

Lily Canyon. As a slight drizzle began, we approached the canyon mouth like the moth does the trumpeting blossom of a desert lily. And yet we had that sad feeling that we were coming to the end of the road, that we were reaching the limits of the canyon country we loved. The Book Cliffs towered above us, but beyond them was an altogether different region. The hawks and owls that have "whitewashed" those cliffs could soar over them and explore that other land, but we would soon have to turn around and go back.

Hawks and owls are not the only ones who have left their marks on these pale sandstone cliffs. Lichens have colored them green and pink. Pour-offs have left dark-streaked watermarks trailing down vertical walls. Still, there are other kinds of paintings that have tinted Lily Canyon's walls, evidence of beings other than rock and hawk and lichen.

Shielded by one massive overhang are red pictographs of the Barrier Canyon style: hollow-eyed, round-shouldered, striped-bodied specters left by an archaic culture present in the area from two to eight thousand years ago. The spirits which haunted ancient hunter-gatherers seem to rise up out of smoke stains on the rock, left by all-night campfires which burned hundreds of generations before ours. These spirits must put some modern residents on edge, for bullet holes now chip at those spooky, hollow eyes. There, on the same sandstone canvas, are three-thousand-year-old Anasazi petroglyphs—bighorn and triangle-torsoed deities, chipped a thousand years ago into even

Human habitation in canyon country goes back at least 11,500 years. The first residents were hunters and gatherers, followed by the pottery-making Fremont and Anasazi, who practiced agriculture and constructed pithouses and cliff dwellings. Fremont and Anasazi ruins, rock art, stone tools, baskets, and pottery are found throughout the slickrock wildlands.

SAND IN THE SOUL
HUMAN IMPRINTS ON CANYON COUNTRY

older red pictographs. The pale peckings of the Wiminuche Ute are alongside them, left as recently as 1870. The Ute still keep a secluded campsite just above the end of the canyon road, so their presence here is not merely historic.

Competing with the Anasazi, Fremont, and Ute for advertising space on the slickrock wall are logos, cattle brands, and signatures of Mormon travelers, ranchers, and farmers from the 1880s through the 1970s. Horses and crosses intermingle with bison and snakes. All these stains, signs, smells, and signatures, from various peoples and their favorite animals, reach back for thousands of years.

Already soaked, we decided to leave the rock art and take a run through the rain, down-canyon, back toward the open desert. The aroma of big sage overpowered the stench of cow dung drenched by the sudden downpour. We ran out onto the Mancos shale, but soon slowed to a walk as our running shoes quickly became caked up with the claylike shale.

The rain passed. Sitting on the damp ground, we tried to scrape the mud off our shoes with twigs and rocks. It came off in little curls almost like wood shavings. We scooped up a few of these clay curls and idly rolled them between our palms into thickened coils that one might use if making a pottery bowl. It was at that moment that we realized that the materials in our hands—wood, stone, and clay—were the three basic raw materials from which our predecessors—Paleo-Indians, Archaic, Anasazi, Fremont, Ute, and Navajo—made everything they needed.

If kept from our modern tools, foods, medicines, and manufactured goods, how would we fare? Could we learn where to find—or when and how to harvest—the 115-some wild food plants that grow on the Colorado Plateau? Of the one hundred twenty forms of wildlife living within a day's reach of this canyon, how many could we catch with arrow, trap, snare, or *atlatl*, the prehistoric missile-propelling weapon? Would we know which trees would make durable utensils, basketry, roof beams, and fuel? And even then, how would we know how to process the wood and bark fiber to make the things we needed?

Prehistoric dwellers on the Colorado Plateau had what archaeologist Bill Lipe calls "a technology of indigenous knowledge"—an orally transmitted tradition of precise scientific knowledge that they depended on for their subsistence. For example, we know that they used at least one hundred thirty-seven different kinds of plants because the remains of that many species have been recovered from archaeological sites on the Colorado Plateau—a testament to the extensive botanical knowledge of indigenous canyon dwellers. The archaeological record has revealed many other examples like this.

* * *

Archaeologists still argue over when human occupation began in canyon country, but most of them agree that people were here at least 11,500 years ago. The first humans, dubbed the Paleo-Indians, had very distinctive tool kits with a variety of fluted, lance-shaped projectile points, perfect for hunting big game. Archaeologists suggest that the nomadic

Although seemingly uninhabitable, deep canyons such as this one along the San Rafael River offered ample resources for prehistoric dwellers.

NAVAJO: THE ATHAPASKAN PATHMAKERS OF THE COLORADO PLATEAU

How long does it take for a people to become "native" to a place? Each of us might answer this question in a different way. But few of us would question that the Dine (Navajo) have finely adapted their way of life to the Colorado Plateau in a matter of just five or six centuries.

When Spanish explorers first encountered Athapaskan people in the American Southwest around 1600, they called them "Apaches del Nabajo." The Tewa Indian term "Nabajo" referred to the people's custom of planting fields, a practice unusual for other Athapaskan or "Apache" groups at the time.

After the Pueblo Revolt of 1680, the Navajo became even more influenced by agricultural peoples who came to live and marry among them. These individuals brought weaving, silversmithing, farming, and dancing traditions with them from the Rio Grande watershed, where the Spanish had gained a foothold. By this time, the dialects of most Navajo clans had diverged from those of other Athapaskan speakers in the Southwest, such as the Jicarilla, the Mescalero, the White Mountain, and other Apache groups to the south and east.

Today, the Navajo are the largest Native American group north of Mexico whose lifestyle is still based on the land. Their population numbers well over two hundred thousand. The twenty-four thousand square miles of land belonging to the Navajo is the largest reservation—or sovereign nation—within U.S. boundaries. There are well over a hundred twenty thousand speakers of their native Athapaskan tongue—a language distinctive enough to have served as an effective secret code during World War II.

The Navajos keep more livestock and weave more wool blankets than any other North American tribe, and much of their land has yielded large quantities of uranium and oil shale. Yet many Navajos are extremely poor by modern economic standards.

Today, Navajos blend the old with the new. Wild roots are still chewed in the shadows of busy fast-food outlets. Medicine men work side by side with young Navajo doctors and nurses conversant with CAT scans, sonograms, and chemotherapies. And computer engineers live alongside elderly, monolingual singers who still chant the ancient oral histories of Athapaskan hunting traditions.

Paleo people, over their span of time here, shifted their reliance on large mammals to smaller game as the centuries went by—no doubt because the population of large game diminished. In fact, these nomadic hunters may have even contributed to the demise of the Ice Age mammals by putting pressure on their populations. These big, woolly, cool-weather animals were already stressed anyway by vegetation changes resulting from a climatic warming trend. By eighty-five hundred years ago, they were history; the so-called Pleistocene extinctions were complete.

With the main sources of their food gone, Paleo-Indians shifted their subsistence strategies. About eighty-five hundred years ago, their old ways were transformed into what archaeologists call the Archaic lifestyle—a new cultural tradition with a different tool kit, found throughout the Southwest. The Archaic people learned to make baskets, atlatls, wooden scoops, clubs, bone tools, cordage, open-twined sandals, and one-handed pestles called *manos*. And yet, even with these new developments, changes in arts and technologies developed slowly over the seven thousand years of the Archaic period.

Then, near the end of the Archaic period, slickrock country inhabitants started experimenting with sowing seeds to increase their food supply and supplement their wild-food gathering. As a result, plants, both wild and domesticated, became more important than ever. The arrival of corn—a monstrously deformed grass traded to people of the north from the wet tropics— must have seemed like a miracle to those familiar with the tiny grains of Indian rice grass and sand dropseed. These more ancient grains are depicted in the rock art panel known as the Harvest Scene, one of the best-preserved depictions of prehistoric food gathering in canyon country.

Suddenly, between 2,250 and 1,500 years ago, the Archaic cultures of the Colorado Plateau were infused with many new crops and creatures, including turkeys and macaws, as well as new technologies, myths, symbols, and ceremonies—all imported from Mexico. These new ideas thrived in some areas but failed in others. Where they took hold, a different civilization was born, known today as the Anasazi.

As they became successful farmers, the Anasazi had time to mold stylized pottery, paint, and make sashes using the treasured Mexican macaw feathers. Their beautiful artwork is found in many places throughout canyon country. They lived in elaborate masonry pueblos, and some areas, like Mesa Verde, had sophisticated irrigation systems. Their Meso-American ties continued to be strong—the "Kokopelli" motif of the humpbacked fluteplayer, for instance, has been linked to the Aztec fertility diety, Xochipilli, a hunched-over, flute-playing musician. The Anasazi culture reached its zenith around 950 to 1150 A.D. not only in the slickrock wildlands of Utah but throughout the Four Corners region, where the southwestern states of Utah, Colorado, Arizona, and New Mexico converge.

At the same time, another group of people, neighbors of the Anasazi called the Fremont, occupied the western part of canyon country—from the west side of the Colorado River to the Great Basin country. The Fremont were not as sophisticated as the Anasazi nor as

*M*onument
Valley is one of the most
scenic areas of the
Navajo Indian
Reservation.

influenced by Meso-American traditions. Even though corn had been introduced to their communities and they had experimented with farming, they ultimately stuck with the old ways, continuing to rely more on hunting and gathering than farming. They had no dogs, turkeys, or macaws, as did the Anasazi. They were inclined to wear animal skin moccasins even when most of their contemporaries had switched to yucca fiber sandals. Even when the Anasazi began to construct masonry buildings, the Fremont continued older traditions of pithouse and brush shelter construction.

Then, in A.D. 1150, a regional drought foreshadowed the periods of stress that both the Anasazi and Fremont would suffer through the next two hundred years. From 1275 to 1300, the drought worsened. Supplies of stored grains and beans were exhausted as food shortages became chronic. Because of falling water tables, Anasazi farmers could no longer irrigate their cultivated crops. In order to rely on prickly pears and other wild foods less affected by droughts, the residents of heavily populated valleys had to leave their large communities and disperse—over three-quarters of all large Anasazi communities were abandoned by 1300. The Fremont people suffered, too, during the drought even though cultivated crops were no longer their mainstay. They, too, moved on.

By 1270, no one was left in the places we presently call Natural Bridges, Glen Canyon, and the Maze. The Anasazi and Fremont cultures, as described here, were gone, marking the end of a great period of human existence in canyon country.

*　*　*

Even though they have been absent now for centuries, the Anasazi and Fremont still haunt the canyons. More than once, when we thought we were alone, we have sensed an unmistakable human presence . . . we look around. Then, across the canyon, we spot something incongruous: square, straight lines, too straight for any lines Mother Nature makes—the dark rectangle of an open window in a cliff dwelling, the ruin itself unnoticeable, melting back into the rock around it. Or, in the canyon, we brush against the Moqui steps—notches in the rock that cradled someone's bare foot as he or she scampered up the cliff face. All along, the human presence we sense is real. We have been walking where others have walked, climbed, farmed, foraged, slept, sang, cried, danced . . . and died.

*　*　*

What happened to the Anasazi and Fremont? Unfortunately, the record is not clear. Chances are their descendants remained in the Southwest after the droughts, with their cultures merely taking new forms as their populations scattered, and they redefined their alliances. However, no one is sure exactly who is descended from whom. Did the Anasazi or Fremont become the Ute or Paiute, Hopi or Zuni? Linguists suggest that the Paiute language was being spoken in southeastern Utah by 1280, and the Utes were certainly evident in the area before the first Spanish explorers arrived in 1765. The Hopi Indians in Arizona are of the same Uto-Aztecan language family as the Ute and southern Paiute. Not surprisingly, one Hopi

WHERE ROCK ART ADORNS THE CANYON WALLS

Pictographs are designs and figures painted on rock with plant and mineral tints. Too much exposure to the sun may cause the painted art to fade. As a result, the best-preserved pictographs lie within shady canyons, beneath protective overhangs.

The ancient petroglyphs and pictographs left on canyon walls attract nearly as many people to the Colorado Plateau as do the canyons themselves. There are at least twelve distinctive styles of rock art that are found in canyon country. They range from the ghostly Barrier Canyon pictographs of human figures and their attendant animals—painted two to four thousand years ago—to the more recent etchings of Ute, Paiute, Navajo, and Mormon. Pictographs were painted on the rock, while petroglyphs were etched into the rock surface, leaving a light-colored image on rock stained dark by desert varnish.

The anthromorphic
Barrier Canyon
pictograph style was
painted with dark red
pigments and buff-
colored tints. Created
by Archaic hunter-
gatherers between
2000 B.C. and 1 A.D.,
these ghostly, tapering
figures are found only
in central and southern
Utah, in the canyons of
the northern Colorado
Plateau.

elder, Walter Hamana, has identified rock art in Natural Bridges National Monument as being from his own tradition: "The ancestors of the Hopi—called the *Hisatsinom*—once inhabited many parts of the American Southwest, including the Natural Bridges area. . . . Throughout their migrations, the Hisatsinom clans left markers to show where they had been."

The little we do know about the indigenous people of the slickrock wildlands after 1300 comes mostly from the oral traditions of the Hopi and Paiute. They have stories about migrations, water holes, salt deposits, major events, animals, and useful plants. Navajo hunters maintain a rich oral tradition about the wildlife of the region. They have never had to rely on sci-entific journals—or even rock art—to transmit their zoological knowledge; they simply tell stories.

That is why one 107-year-old Navajo man, Hastiin Bikeni, began to worry when he realized that such stories about animals and traditional ways were becoming scarce.

"Someday," Bikeni warned us, "People will begin to ask questions [like], 'Let's see, how was it? What was it? What was its name?' These are the kind of stories that need to be told. . . . These are the kinds of stories the people used to tell each other. . . . This is what carried us so far."

We remember a time recently when we visited a Navajo farmer near the south-ern edge of canyon country. There, in a place where farming had been abandoned years before and tumbleweeds had taken over, a wiry, old Navajo man developed a novel way of farming, using a combination of traditional Navajo dryland methods with modern, solar-powered pump-ing technologies. His solar-powered pump not only lifted water from the shallow stream in the downcut arroyo forty feet below his field, but also passed the water through filters that reduced the salt content of the highly mineralized flow. He could then use the purified water to irrigate traditional, native varieties of corn, squashes, and herbs as well as hardy introductions of peaches and other fruits. What fascinated us about this Navajo farmer, who spoke only his native Athapaskan tongue, was that he had integrated ancient ways with the most modern. Clearly, he was going to use whatever worked best, without depleting his resources.

* * *

Anyone wanting a lasting relationship with canyon country, a sustainable rela-tionship that neither depletes nor destroys, can let a little of its grittiness shape them as it has shaped our Navajo friend. The tough Mormon pioneers who settled on slickrock in the 1870s are fine examples of people who have been inextricably shaped by the country they chose. They adapted to the scale, sand, and seasonality of this country, rather than trying to remake Utah to be like the places they had come from. The Fremont adapted, too. So did the Anasazi. Caroline's father used to smile whenever he saw an old-timer who had obviously lived a good life in this country and had let it change him, rather than the other way around. Bates would simply say, "That fella has a little sand in his soul." He could bestow no higher compliment on another human being.

Handprints mark the canyon wall above the ruins of a circular maize granary. Seeds were often hermetically sealed within pottery jars and placed within gra-naries, such as this one, to preserve them for future planting.

MORMON FARMERS AND RANCHERS:
LATTER-DAY SLICKROCK DWELLERS

There had been other European-Americans who had penetrated farther, deeper, and earlier into slickrock country than the Mormon settlers: Juan Maria Antonio de Rivera in 1765; the missionaries Dominguez-Velez and Escalante in 1776; the enigmatic fur trader, Dennis Julien, between 1836 and 1847; and the visionary John Wesley Powell in 1869. But once the Mormons established their footholds in the slickrock wildlands, which they had done by 1849, they cultivated a community with deep roots in Utah's canyon country.

Arriving mostly from New York, Illinois, and Missouri, determined Mormons, members of The Church of Jesus Christ of Latter-Day Saints, settled in the canyons and mountains of Utah, seeking religious freedom. In the mid-1850s, a few of the early Mormon settlements in southern Utah had to be abandoned as a result of Indian skirmishes. But twenty years later, well-kept Mormon towns and productive orchards had been solidly established throughout Utah, where they are still found today.

A line camp in Escalante country is testimony to hard times and life on the fringes of civilization.

ACKNOWLEDGMENTS

Among the slickrock aficionados who offered us hospitality, libraries, great stories, general support, and cool swims, we would like to thank: Lloyd and Marian Pierson, Mary and Mitch Williams, Edie Wilson, Dudley Beck, Julie Beck, Peter Lawson, Anne Wilson, and Andy Nettell. The late Robin Wilson and Tug Wilson, Stewart Udall, Mitch Williams, Lloyd Pierson, Jane Belnap, Ginger Harmon, Bruce Hucko, Susan and Ann Zwinger, Tom Fleischner, Stephen Trimble, Jose Knighton, Julio Betancourt, Jack Turner, Phil Hyde, and Barney Burns provided special perspectives and inspiration regarding the human history and appropriate use of the canyon country. We wish to acknowledge the kindness and insights offered to us throughout this project by National Park Service, Bureau of Land Management, The Nature Conservancy, and National Biological Survey employees who are lucky enough to live and work in the canyon country, including Jane Belnap, Nancy Coulam, Andy Nettell, Sue Bellagama, Diane Allen, Larry Frederick, Jim Dougan, Rick Nolan, Stephanie Dubois, John Spence, John Rittenouer, Riley Mitchell, Allyson Mathis, Judie Chrobak-Cox, Francis Rakow, and Tara Williams. A number of folks were also patient enough to read our manuscript and offer their review comments—to them, a big thanks: Nancy Coulam, Jane Belnap, Lloyd Pierson, John Spence, Tara Williams, Fred Peterson, David Williams, Don Baars, Hellmut Doelling, Lehi Hintze, Bill Dickenson, Steve Trimble, and Edie Wilson. Thanks to many other people who provided us with fresh technical or historical information, including: Tim Graham, Fred Peterson, Don Baars, Ned Colbert, Bill Breed, Deb Westfall, Lisa Floyd-Hanna, Margaret Hopkin, Jose Knighton, and Ben Jones. Our special thanks to John Williams and Gary Heinze at NAVTEC for a great river trip and to David Williams for a wonderful geological field trip. Dusty and Laura Nabhan and Ginger Harmon accompanied us on camping trips, hikes, and river trips. Victoria Shoemaker was our agent and wise advisor in this book; to her we are very grateful. Lastly, we would like to thank the Tehabi team: Tom, Susan, Nancy, Sam, Andy, Sharon and Chris, who stuck with us over the humps, bumps and detours. We are especially glad that we were able to spend time with Jeff Garton in the field; we now have an even better appreciation of his fine photos.

GARY PAUL NABHAN AND CAROLINE COALTER WILSON
Three Points, Arizona

Many thanks to Gary Nabhan and Caroline Wilson for sharing their wealth of knowledge of biota and geology, which deepened my understanding of ecosystems in canyon country; to Escalante Park Service rangers Jim Bowman and Bill Wolverton for advice and assistance on remote backcountry treks, and to Henry Wood for the use of his refrigerator; and to hiking companions Todd Tiffan, Ethan Brown, and Max and Maxine Hollenbeck. And to my wife, Melissa Louise, my greatest gratitude and appreciation.

JEFF GARTON
Tucson, Arizona

NOTE: Throughout this book, as part of efforts to preserve Utah's slickrock wildlands, we have refrained from mentioning the names and exact locations of the sites of archaeological ruins and other fragile resources which should receive only limited, controlled visitation.

INDEX

SELECTED BIBLIOGRAPHY

BETWEEN CLIFF WALLS

Abbey, Edward, *Desert Solitaire*, University of Arizona Press, Tucson, 1988

Cannon, Helen L., *The Development of Botanical Methods of Prospecting for Uranium on the Colorado Plateau*, U.S. Geological Survey Bulletin 1085-A, Atomic Energy Commission, U.S. Government Printing Office, Washington, D.C., 1960

Comstock, Jonathan P. and Ehleringer, James R., "Plant Adaptation in the Great Basin and Colorado Plateau," *Great Basin Naturalist 52 (3)*: 195–215, 1992

Cronquist, Arthur, Holmgren, Arthur H., Holmgren, Noel H., and Reveal, James L., *Intermountain Flora: Vascular Plants of the Intermountain West*, New York Botanical Garden/Hafner Publishing Company, New York, 1972

Frost, Kent, *My Canyonlands*, Aberlard-Schuman, New York, 1971

LAYER UPON LAYER and WHERE WATER RULES

Abbey, Edward and Hyde, Philip, *Slickrock: Endangered Canyons of the Southwest*, Sierra Club/Charles Scribner's Sons, New York, 1971

Allen, Steve, *Canyoneering: The San Rafael Swell*, University of Utah Press, Salt Lake City, 1992

Baars, Donald L., *Canyonlands Country: Geology of Canyonlands and Arches National Parks*, Canyonlands Natural History Association, Moab, 1989

Baars, Donald L., *The Colorado Plateau: A Geologic History*, University of New Mexico Press, Albuquerque, 1983

Chronic, Halka, *Pages of Stone: Geology of Western National Parks and Monuments*, The Mountaineers, Seattle, 1988

Colbert, Edwin H., "Historical Aspects of the Triassic-Jurassic Boundary Problem," Kevin Padian, ed., *The Beginning of the Age of Dinosaurs*, Cambridge University Press, Cambridge, 1986

Collier, Michael, *The Geology of Capitol Reef National Park*, Capitol Reef Natural History Association/Lorraine Press, Salt Lake City, 1987

Cooke, Ronald U. and Warren, Andrew, *Geomorphology in Deserts*, University of California Press, Berkeley, 1973

Doelling, Hellmut H., *Geology of Arches National Park*, Utah Geological and Mineral Survey, Salt Lake City, 1985

Doelling, Hellmut H., *Map 74—Geologic Map of Arches National Park and Vicinity, Grand County, Utah*, Utah Geological and Mineral Survey, Salt Lake City, 1985

Doelling, Hellmut H., Oviatt, Charles G., and Huntoon, Peter W., *Salt Deformation in the Paradox Region*, Utah Geological and Mineral Survey Bulletin 122, Salt Lake City, 1988

Hintze, Lehi F., *Geologic History of Utah*, Brigham Young University Geology Studies Special Publication 7, Provo, 1988

Hintze, Lehi F., *Geological Highway Map of Utah*, Brigham Young University Geology Studies Special Publication 3, Provo, 1992

Huntoon, Peter W., Billingsley, George H., and Breed, William J., *Geologic Map of Canyonlands National Park and Vicinity, Utah*, Canyonlands Natural History Association, Moab, 1982

Lohman, S.W., *The Geologic Story of Arches National Park*, U.S. Geological Survey Bulletin 1393, U.S. Government Printing Office, Washington, D.C., 1980

Loope, David B., "Eolian Origin of Upper Paleozoic Sandstones, Southeastern Utah," *Journal of Sedimentary Petrology 54 (2)*: 563–580, 1984

Loope, David B., "Abandonment of the Name 'Elephant Canyon Formation' in Southeastern Utah: Physical and Temporal Implications," *The Mountain Geologist 27 (4)*: 119–130, 1990

Rigby, Keith J., "Stratigraphy and Structure of the San Rafael Reef, Utah; A Major Monocline of the Colorado Plateau," *Geological Society of America Centennial Field Guide - Rocky Mountain Section 100*: 269–273, 1987

Stokes, William Lee, *Geology of Utah*, Utah Museum of Natural History Occasional Paper Number 6, Salt Lake City, 1986

INTO EVERY CREVICE

Belnap, Jane, Harper, Kimball T., and Warren, Steven D., "Surface Disturbance of Cryptobiotic Soil Crusts: Nitrogenase Activity, Chlorophyll Content, and Chlorophyll Degradation," *Arid Soil and Research 8*: 1–8, 1993

Belnap, Jane, "Potential Role of Cryptobiotic Soil Crusts in Semiarid Rangelands," *Symposium on Ecology, Management, and Restoration of Intermountain Annual Rangelands*, USDA Forest Service Intermountain Research Station, Boise, 1992

Belnap, Jane and Gardner, John S., "Soil Microstructure in Soils of the Colorado Plateau: The Role of the Cyanobacterium *Microcoleus vaginatus*," *Great Basin Naturalist 53 (1)*: 40–47, 1993

Belnap, Jane, "Recovery Rates of Cryptobiotic Crusts: Inoculant Use and Assessment Methods," *Great Basin Naturalist 53 (1)*: 89–95, 1993

Betancourt, Julio L., Van Devender, Thomas R., and Martin, Paul S., *Packrat Middens: The Last 40,000 Years of Biotic Change*, University of Arizona Press, Tucson, 1990

Bowers, Janice E., "The Plant Ecology of Inland Dunes in Western North America," *Journal of Arid Environments 5 (3)*: 199–220, 1982

Cannon, Helen L. and Starrett, W. H., *Botanical Prospecting for Uranium on La Ventana Mesa, Sandoval County, New Mexico*, U.S. Geological Survey Bulletin 1009-M, U.S. Government Printing Office, Washington D,C., 1956

Cole, David N., "Trampling Disturbance and Recovery of Cryptogamic Soil Crusts in Grand Canyon National Park," *Great Basin Naturalist 50 (4)*: 321–325, 1990

Everitt, Benjamin L., *A Survey of the Desert Vegetation of the Northern Henry Mountains Region, Hanksville, Utah*, Johns Hopkins University Ph.D. dissertation, Washington, D.C. 1970

Fagan, Damian, *Plant List - Arches National Park*, Canyonlands Natural History Association, Moab, 1991

Froelich, Albert J. and Kleinhampl, Frank J., *Botanical Prospecting for Uranium in the Deer Flat Area, White Canyon District, San Juan County, Utah*, U.S. Geological Survey Bulletin 1085-B, U.S. Government Printing Office, Washington, D.C., 1960

Heil, Kenneth D., Floyd-Hanna, Lisa, Reeves, Linda, Hyder, Don, and Fleming, Richard, *Habitat Requirements of Endangered, Threatened and Rare Plant Species in the Southeast Utah Group of National Parks*, San Juan College, Farmington, 1993

Meyer, Susan E., *Places in the Sun: Story of Capitol Reef Plants*, Capitol Reef Natural History Association/Lorraine Press, Salt Lake City, 1990

Potter, Loren D., Reynolds, Robert C., and Louderbough, Ellen T., "Mancos Shale and Plant Community Relationships: Analysis of Shale, Soil and Vegetation Transects," *Journal of Arid Environments 9 (2)*: 147-166, 1985

Potter, Loren D., Reynolds, Robert C., and Louderbough, Ellen T., "Mancos Shale and Plant Community Relationships: Field Observations," *Journal of Arid Environments 9 (2)*: 137–146, 1985

Sharpe, Saxon E., *Late Pleistocene and Holocene Vegetation Change in Arches National Park, Grand County, Utah, and Dinosaur National Monument, Moffet County, Colorado*, Masters Thesis, Northern Arizona University, Flagstaff, 1991

Spence, John R. and Henderson, Norman R., "Tinaja and Hanging Garden Vegetation of Capitol Reef National Park, Southern Utah, U.S.A.," *Journal of Arid Environments 24 (1)*: 21–37, 1993

Van Pelt, Nicholas S., *Woodland Parks in Southeastern Utah*, Masters Thesis, University of Utah, Salt Lake City, 1978

Welsh, Stanley L., Atwood, Duane N., Goodrich, Sherel, and Higgins, Larry C., "A Utah Flora," *Great Basin Naturalist Memoirs 9*: 1–894, 1987

Welsh, Stanley L. "On the Distribution of Utah's Hanging Gardens," *Great Basin Naturalist 49 (1)*: 1–30, 1989

CARVING A NICHE

Armstrong, David M., *Mammals of the Canyon Country*, Canyonlands Natural History Association, Moab, 1982

Betancourt, Julio, Pierson, Elizabeth A., Rylander, Kate Aasen, Fairchild-Parks, James A., and Dean, Jeffery S., "Influence of History and Climate on New Mexico Pinyon-Juniper Woodlands," *Symposium on Managing Pinyon-Juniper Ecosystems for Sustainability and Social Needs*, USDA Forest Service Rocky Mountain Forest and Range Experiment Station General Technical Report RM-236, Fort Collins, 1993

Brazell, Ricky E., Workman, Gar W., and May, David D., *A Preliminary Survey on Beaver (Castor canadensis) in Canyonlands National Park, Utah*, Utah State Department of Wildlife Science, Logan, 1977

Brown, David E., "Biotic Communities of the American Southwest: United States and Mexico," *Desert Plants 4 (1–4)*: 1–342, 1982

Brown, James H. and Heske, Edward J., "Control of a Desert-Grassland Transition by a Keystone Rodent Guild," **Science 250**: 1705–1707, 1990

Clark, Tim W., Campbell, Thomas M., Socha, David G., and Casey, Denise E., "Prairie Dog Colony Attributes and Associated Vertebrate Species," *Great Basin Naturalist 42 (4)*: 572–582, 1982

Floyd, Lisa and Kohler, Timothy A., "Current Productivity and Prehistoric Use of Piñon (*Pinus edulis*, Pinaceae) in the Dolores Archaeological Project Area, Southwestern Colorado," *Economic Botany 44 (2)*: 141–156, 1990

Hawkins, Lauraine K. and Nicoletto, Paul F., "Kangaroo Rat Burrows Structure: The Spatial Organization of Ground-dwelling Animals in a Semiarid Grassland," *Journal of Arid Environments 23 (4)*: 199–208, 1992

Neilson, Ronald P. and Wullstein, L.H., "Microhabitat Affinities of Gambel Oak Seedlings," *Great Basin Naturalist 46 (2)*: 294–298, 1986

Nettoff, Dennis, *Morphology and Possible Origin of the Giant Weathering Pits in the Entrada Sandstone at Rock Creek Bay, Glen Canyon National Recreation Area, Southeastern Utah*, Sam Houston State University Grant Proposal, Huntsville, 1993

Trimble, Stephen, *The Sagebrush Ocean: A Natural History of the Great Basin*, University of Nevada Press, Reno, 1989

Van Pelt, Nicholas S. and Johnson, David W., "Isolated Butte and Mesa Summits of the Colorado Plateau," *Symposium on Managing Pinyon-Juniper Ecosystems for Sustainability and Social Needs*, USDA Forest Service Rocky Mountain Forest and Range Experiment Station General Technical Report RM-236, Fort Collins, 1993

SAND IN THE SOUL

Barnes, Fran, *Canyonlands National Park - Early History and First Descriptions*, Another Canyon Country Guidebook 16, Canyon Country Publications, Moab, 1988

Cutler, Hugh C., *Corn, Cucurbits, and Cotton from Glen Canyon*, University of Utah Department of Anthropology Anthropological Papers 80, Salt Lake City, 1966

Dean, Jeffrey S., Euler, Robert C., Gumerman, George J., Plog, Fred, Hevly, Richard H., and Karlstrom, Thor N.V., "Human Behavior, Demography, and Paleoenvironment of the Colorado Plateau," *American Antiquity 50 (3)*: 537–554, 1985

Grayson, Donald K., *The Desert's Past: A Natural Prehistory of the Great Basin*, Smithsonian Institution Press, Washington, D.C., 1993

Grey, Ralph, "Livestock Reduction and Other Experiences," excerpted in *Blue Mountain Shadows 11*: 1, 1992

Jennings, Jesse D., *Cowboy Cave*, University of Utah Anthropological Papers 104, Salt Lake City, 1980

Lavender, David, *Colorado River Country*, E. F. Dutton Press, New York, 1982

Madsen, David B., *Exploring the Fremont*, Utah Museum of Natural History, Salt Lake City, 1989

Parker, Kathleene, *The Only True People: A History of the Native Americans of the Colorado Plateau*, Thunder Mesa Publishing, Denver, 1991

Sims, Richard, "Stories from the Land," *Plateau 53 (2)*, Museum of Northern Arizona, 1981

Tipps, Betsy L. and Hewitt, Nancy J., "Cultural Resource Inventory and Testing in the Salt Creek Pocket and Devils Lane Areas, Needles District, Canyonlands National Park, Utah," National Park Service Rocky Mountain Region, *Cultural Resources Report 411-01-8827*, 1989

Trimble, Stephen, *The People - Indians of the American Southwest*, School of American Research, Santa Fe, 1993